D0184260

ABC OF CHILD ABUSE

ABC OF CHILD ABUSE

edited by

ROY MEADOW FRCP

Professor of Paediatrics and Child Health, St James's University Hospital, Leeds

with contributions by

FRANK BAMFORD, SYLVIA FRASER, C J HOBBS, JILL McMURRAY, BARBARA MITCHELS,
A R NICOL, RAINE ROBERTS, DAVID H SKUSE, NIGEL SPEIGHT

Articles published in
the *British Medical Journal*

Published by the British Medical Journal
Tavistock Square, London WC1H 9JR

© British Medical Journal 1989

First published 1989

British Library Cataloguing in Publication Data

Meadow, Roy
  ABC of child abuse
  1. Children. Abuse by adults
  I. Title
  361.7'044

ISBN 0-7279-0258-X

Printed in Great Britain by Jolly & Barber Ltd, Rugby
Typesetting by Bedford Typesetters Ltd, Bedford

Contents

EPIDEMIOLOGY

Roy Meadow

This week at least four children in Britain will die as a result of abuse or neglect. This year most departments of social services and of child health will be notified of more than 20 times as many cases of suspected child abuse as they were 10 years ago. Although some of the reports will prove to be unfounded, the common experience is that proved cases of child abuse are four or five times as common as they were a decade ago. The names of nearly 40 000 children in England are listed on child protection (at risk) registers. This poses enormous burdens on staff in the health and social services and raises many problems about the lives and welfare of children in our society today. Determining whether there is a true increase of child abuse or whether the figures merely reflect increased awareness rests to some extent on the definition of child abuse.

Definition

A child is considered to be abused if he or she is treated by an adult in a way that is unacceptable in a given culture at a given time. The last two clauses are important because not only are children treated differently in different countries but within a country, and even within a city, there are subcultures of behaviour and variations of opinion about what constitutes abuse of children. Moreover, standards obviously change

over the years: corporal punishment has become significantly less acceptable in Britain in the past 10 years. Looking back further there is evidence that the abuse of children by parents was considered to be culturally acceptable in Britain 100 years ago. At the time that Lord Shaftesbury was creating better conditions for children at work he was unwilling to tackle the problem of child abuse at home.

> The evils are enormous and indisputable, but they are so private, internal and domestic a character as to be beyond the reach of legislation and the subject would not, I think, be entertained in either House of Parliament.
> LORD SHAFTESBURY, 1880

In fact the first charter for children appeared in 1889, some 67 years after the introduction of legislation to protect animals.

Types of abuse

Physical abuse (non-accidental injury)—The prototype of physical abuse, "the battered baby," was rediscovered by Henry Kempe of Denver, Colorado, in 1962 and has been well publicised ever since. Physical abuse entails soft tissue injury to the skin, eyes, ears, and internal organs as well as to ligaments and bones. Burns and scalds are included. Most of this abuse is short

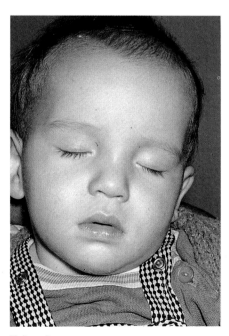

Poisoning

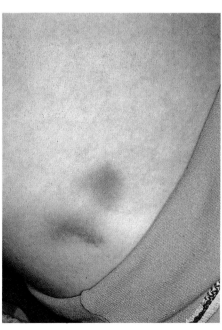

Pinching

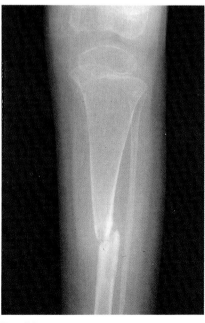

Breaking

1

Epidemiology

Punching

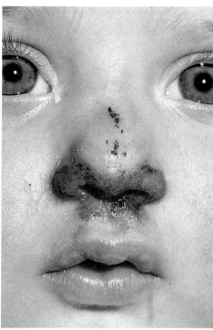

Slapping

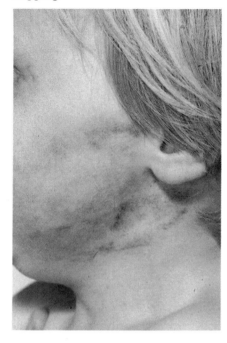

Lashing

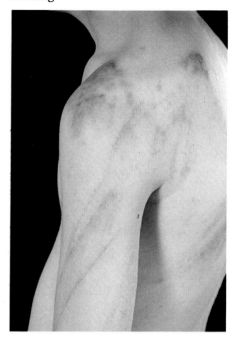

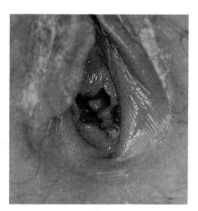

Raping

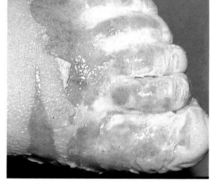

Scalding

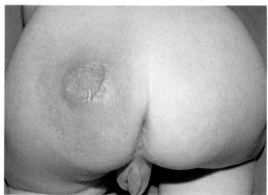

Burning

term and violent, though it may be repetitive. There is, however, a subgroup that entails more long term deliberate injury, including poisoning and suffocation.

Neglect—This is failing to provide the love, care, food, or physical circumstances that will allow a child to grow and develop normally. Or it is exposing a child to any kind of danger.

Sexual abuse—This occurs when dependent, developmentally immature children and adolescents participate in sexual activities that they do not fully comprehend, to which they are unable to give informed consent, and that violate the social taboos of family roles. Such abuse ranges from inappropriate fondling and masturbation to intercourse and buggery. Children may also be forced to participate in producing pornographic pictures by photography or video.

Emotional abuse—This has no generally agreed definition. Some regard a child as abused if he or she has a behavioural disturbance to which the parents fail to respond appropriately in terms of modifying their behaviour or seeking

professional help. Most would consider a child to be emotionally abused, however, if the child's behaviour and emotional development were severely affected by the parents' persistent neglect or rejection. Thus emotional abuse may lead to a failure to thrive and short stature in young children. Other less common forms of emotional abuse include the Munchausen syndrome by proxy, in which the parents force the child into a role of inappropriate illness.

Commonly, different types of abuse overlap with each other so a child may be being abused in several different ways either at the same time or sequentially.

Clearly, in most forms of abuse the abuser, usually the parent, may harm the child both actively and passively and by acts of both commission and omission. One parent may be active in beating the child, another just as harmful by passively failing to protect a child from the sexual advances of a cohabitant. A parent who passively fails to provide food or love for a child may indulge also in active physical assault.

Starving   Cutting   Buggering

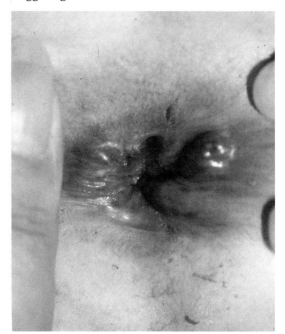

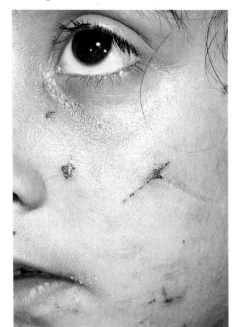

Prevalence

Four per cent of children up to the age of 12 are brought to the notice of professional agencies (social service departments or the National Society for the Prevention of Cruelty to Children) because of suspected abuse. Some of that abuse is not proved and some of it is mild, but a British survey has shown that each year at least one child per 1000 under the age of 4 years suffers severe physical abuse—for example, fractures, brain haemorrhage, severe internal injuries, or mutilation. A minimum mortality is one in 10 000 children; most people concerned with child abuse believe the mortality to be considerably higher as many cases are undetected.

The prevalence of other types of abuse is even more difficult to determine. Much depends upon how the abuse is defined and whether minor degrees of abuse are included in a study. This problem is particularly apparent in sexual abuse.

Most adults can probably remember an unpleasant sexual event or inappropriate approach that was made to them as a child, but if it was merely someone who indulged in indecent exposure on one occasion or fumbled about his or her clothing they probably do not consider that they have been sexually abused. Most reported instances of sexual abuse do not entail physical contact; abuse entailing physical contact, in terms of attempted or actual intercourse, is likely to be more important and certainly causes more concern. Many of the recent mass surveys have failed to distinguish between different types of abuse or to deal with the severity or repetition of the abuse. Moreover, the authors sometimes seem to forget the limitations of adults reporting past sexual experiences, particularly if they are doing so at a time of emotional upset (perhaps

Freud's writings of 80 years ago should be compulsory reading for all research workers). Home Office criminal statistics yield merely a few hundred cases a year of sexual abuse of children and grossly underrepresent the true incidence, tending more to reflect detection skills and prosecution practice. The National Society for the Prevention of Cruelty to Children reported a yearly incidence of sexual abuse in 1986 of 0·57 cases per 1000 children. This figure was based on the number of children entered on to child protection registers because of sexual abuse that year. It reflects the degree of suspicion at that time and the practices of the local authorities keeping the child abuse registers: it does not give any indication of the type or severity of the abuse.

Thus, although there is some evidence that there may have been an increase in some forms of child abuse in the past five years, the current escalation of reported cases and identified cases is much more a matter of public awareness, better professional recognition, and an unwillingness by society to tolerate the abuse of children.

In April 1988, 39 300 children were thought to be on child protection registers in England, a rate of 3·5 children per 1000 population below the age of 18 years. More than a quarter of the children on the registers were in the care of local authorities, and another 10% were subject to supervision orders.

Child protection registers

Main reason for child being placed on register (1988)

Grave concern	34%
Physical abuse	25%
Sexual abuse	13%
Neglect	13%
Other reasons	15%

Aetiology

Boys and girls are both abused. First born children are more often affected, and within a family it is common for just one of the children to be abused and the others to be free from such abuse. Young children are most at risk, partly because they are more vulnerable and partly because they cannot seek help elsewhere. Children under 2 years of age are most at risk from severe physical abuse. Death from abuse is rare after the age of 1 year.

Most abuse is by the child's parents, and it is particularly common for a parent or cohabitant who is living in the home but is not related to the child to be the abuser. Young parents are more likely to abuse than older ones. Abusing parents usually do not have an identified mental illness, though many show personality traits predisposing to violent behaviour or inappropriate sexual behaviour. Child abuse is more likely in those who are socially deprived and in families without employment, but it is most important to recognise that it occurs in all layers of society.

Abuse is thought to be 20 times more likely if one of the parents was abused as a child. Though there is a strong tendency for those who were abused to abuse their own children in turn, more than a third of mothers abused as children nevertheless provide good care for their children and do not abuse them.

Awareness of the commonness of child abuse is an important step towards its recognition. The other necessary requirement is for doctors and nurses to be aware of the awful variety of ways in which children are abused. We can all understand the way in which a weary parent strikes an exasperating child but many normal people are too decent to imagine the degree of depravity, violence, cruelty, and cunning associated with child abuse. It is necessary to be aware of these wilder limits because we can recognise and manage disorders only if we know about them from either experience or teaching. The articles that follow will deal with both the common and the less common forms of child abuse.

Further reading

Kempe CH, Silverman FN, Steele BF, Droegmuller W, Silver HK. The battered-child syndrome. *JAMA* 1962;**181**:17-24.

Finkelhor D, Korbin J. Child abuse as an international issue. *Child Abuse Negl* 1988;**12**:3-23.

Creighton SJ. The incidence of child abuse and neglect. In: Browne K, Davies C, Stratton P, eds. *Early prediction and prevention of child abuse.* Chichester: Wiley, 1988.

Widom CS. Sampling biases and implications for child abuse research. *Am J Orthopsychiatry* 1988;**58**:260-70.

Markowe HLJ. The frequency of childhood sexual abuse in the UK. *Health Trends* 1988;**1**(Feb):2-6.

NON-ACCIDENTAL INJURY

Nigel Speight

> **Child abuse is the difference between a hand on the bottom and a fist in the face.**
>
> HENRY KEMPE

Difficulty of diagnosis

The diagnosis of physical abuse (non-accidental injury) is a difficult intellectual and emotional exercise. It is one of the most difficult subjects in clinical work, needing time, experience, and emotional energy. The biggest barrier to diagnosis is the existence of emotional blocks in the minds of professionals. These can be so powerful that they prevent the diagnosis even being considered in quite obvious cases (see, for example, case 1).

All those working with children should be warned that their overwhelming impulse on confronting their first case will be to want to cover it up.

The most important step in diagnosing non-accidental injury is to force yourself to think of it in the first place.

Importance of diagnosis

Non-accidental injury is one of the most important diagnoses in clinical paediatrics as it can so vitally influence a child's future life. At worst it is a matter of life and death for the child, and short of death there may still be possible brain damage or handicap. Though high risk cases are currently in a minority, the diagnosis remains crucially important in every case. This is because non-accidental injury is often a marker for emotional abuse and deprivation that can cause progressive and possibly permanent damage to a child's developing personality. This principle is especially relevant in children of school age. In such children the risk of death may be extremely small, yet non-accidental injury in older children is almost inevitably associated with a longstanding disturbance of the parent-child relationship. For this reason non-accidental injury should never be dismissed as "overchastisement."

Non-accidental injury is not a full diagnosis, it is merely a symptom of disordered parenting. The aim of intervention is to diagnose and cure (if possible) the disordered parenting. Simply to aim at preventing death is a lowly ambition.

In some cases the occurrence of physical abuse may provide an opportunity for intervention. If this opportunity is missed there may be no further opportunity for many years.

Diagnostic features

There are no hard and fast rules and no easy answers for diagnosis. The following list constitutes seven classic "pointers" to the diagnosis. None of them is diagnostic, neither does the absence of any of them exclude the diagnosis of non-accidental injury.

(1) There is a delay in seeking medical help (or medical help is not sought at all).

(2) The story of the "accident" is vague, is lacking in detail, and may vary with each telling and from person to person. (Innocent accidents tend to have vivid accounts that ring true.)

(3) The account of the accident is not compatible with the injury observed.

(4) The parents' affect is abnormal. Normal parents are full of creative anxiety for the child. Abusing parents tend to be more preoccupied with their own problems—for example, how they can return home as soon as possible.

(5) The parents' behaviour gives cause for

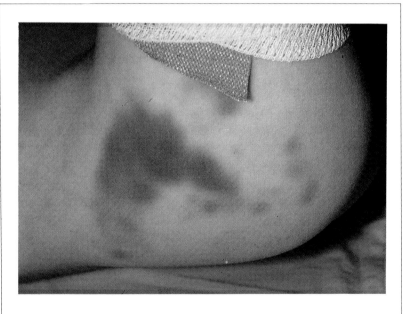

Case 1: The importance of what the child says

This 4 year old girl had been "rehabilitated" under a care order eight months previously. She was brought to hospital with a fractured femur. Her father claimed that she had fallen down stairs, and despite the excessive bruising on her thigh and buttocks and her abject appearance no questions were asked. The next morning she told a nurse, "Daddy told Mummy he would never do it again." On further questioning the father became aggressive and had to be restrained by police from abducting the child after attempting to remove her Gallow's traction.

Case 2: The importance of the child's appearance

These pictures show the "before and after" effect when severe deprivation is reversed. This 3 year old boy was in fact never subjected to non-accidental injury, but many children in cases of non-accidental injury may have the same appearance. He was admitted after a genuine accident and noted to be extremely deprived. The bond between him and his mother was non-existent. (He had been admitted two years before with non-organic failure to thrive and retardation but allowed to lapse from medical follow up with no referral to social services.) In the ward he showed noticeable affection-seeking behaviour and flourished. The follow up photograph was taken six months later while he was in foster care.

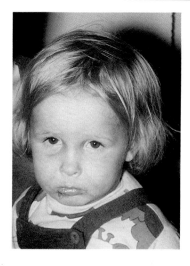 

concern—for example, they soon become hostile, they rebut accusations that have not been made, and they leave before the consultant arrives.

(6) The child's appearance and his interaction with his parents are abnormal. He may look sad, withdrawn, or frightened (case 2). There may be visible evidence of a failure to thrive. Full blown frozen watchfulness is a late stage and results from repetitive physical and emotional abuse over a period of time. The absence of frozen watchfulness does not exclude the diagnosis of non-accidental injury.

(7) The child may say something (case 1). Always make a point of interviewing the child (if old enough) in a safe place in private. This is one of the virtues of admission to hospital. Interviewing the child as an outpatient may fail to let the child open up as he is expecting to be returned to the custody of the abusing parent in the near future.

Characteristic patterns of injury

Some forms of injury are by their nature virtually diagnostic of non-accidental injury. These include finger tip bruising, especially when it is multiple (cases 3 and 4); cigarette burns; lash marks (case 5); retinal and subdural haemorrhages (figure), which can occur after a shaking injury without other evidence of bruising or fracture; and a torn frenulum.

How to approach a case of suspected non-accidental injury

Firstly, approach the parents as you would in any other clinical case. Introduce yourself, shake hands, and proceed logically through the history, examination, provisional diagnosis, and decision making.

Secondly, do not jump to conclusions one way or the other. Try to proceed slowly and deliberately, keeping your mind open as long as possible. Take a provisional social history to form a picture of the family's background and how likely it would be for abuse to occur there.

Referral pathway

The diagnosis of non-accidental injury is a two tier exercise. The doctor on the front line (general practitioner, senior house officer in the accident and emergency department, or school doctor) is responsible for identifying children with suspected physical abuse and referring them to a consultant paediatrician for definitive diagnosis.

Role of front line doctors

Doctors on the front line must realise and accept the limits of their responsibility. They do not have to make a definitive diagnosis and should have a comparatively low threshold of referral. It should be accepted that some children

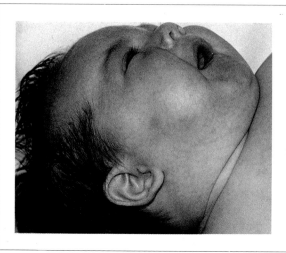

Case 3: Finger tip bruising and fractured ribs

This 4 month old baby was noted to have two bruises on the cheek highly suggestive of finger tip bruising from forceful gripping. A skeletal survey showed two healing rib fractures caused by an episode four to eight weeks previously.

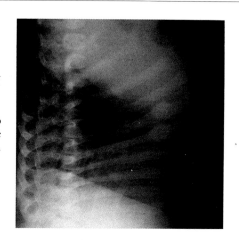

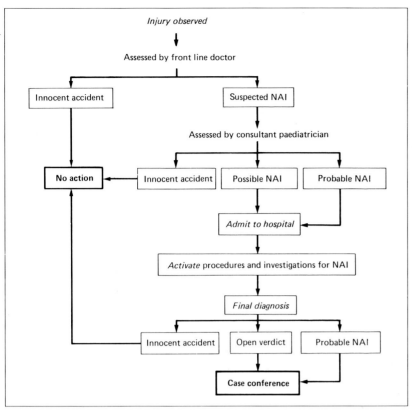

Flow chart for referral of cases of suspected non-accidental injury (NAI)

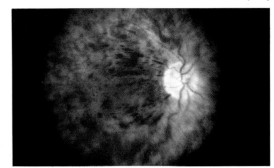

Retinal haemorrhage from non-accidental injury

with innocent injuries will be referred. If all of the children referred turn out to have been physically abused the threshold for referral is almost certainly too high.

Front line doctors should not feel guilt about referring children with suspected non-accidental injury to a paediatrician. They are not accusing either parent; they are simply asking for a second opinion on an important and difficult diagnosis. The fact that the child is being referred because of suspected non-accidental injury should be conveyed to the parents in a neutral and matter of fact way. It is not in the interests of children or parents for child abuse to be covered up. To do so leaves the parents at greater risk of inflicting more severe injuries next time, being imprisoned for causing more severe injuries, and losing long term custody of their children. Early intervention may help to prevent these events.

It is the duty of front line doctors to refer all children with suspected non-accidental injury. Failing to do so is a form of professional negligence. In the United States failing to report suspected child abuse is a federal offence punishable by imprisonment.

Role of the consultant paediatrician

It is vital to the interests of the child, the parents, and all the professionals concerned that the paediatrician reaches a correct and definite diagnosis in as many cases as possible. (This duty should not be delegated to junior staff.) If the paediatrician sits on the fence he or she will not only be in an uncomfortable position but also be doing a disservice to the child and the parents. If the paediatrician finds it impossible to decide initially he or she should admit the child to hospital while investigations continue. Few cases are uncertain after a thorough multidisciplinary investigation. The paediatrician should remember that he or she is being asked to commit himself or herself only on the balance of probabilities—not beyond all reasonable doubt. If the paediatrician genuinely cannot decide between non-accidental injury and an innocent injury, he or she should return an open verdict and decisions should be guided by the psychosocial assessment.

I thank the medical illustration units at the Royal Victoria Infirmary and Newcastle General Hospital for their help, particularly Mr Peter Grencis, medical photographer at Dryburn Hospital.

Case 4: Finger tip bruising

This 2 year old boy was admitted with a fractured tibia, bruising to the face, and classic finger tip bruising over the right scapula.

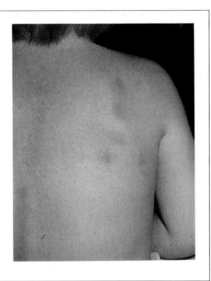

Case 5: Lash marks

This 10 year old girl was whipped with a belt by her depressed father. The linear nature of the marks is seen, together with a tramlining effect, in which the point of impact is white and the adjoining skin shows bruising caused by capillaries that have been broken by blood being forced into them.

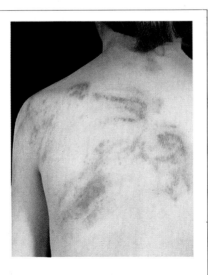

FRACTURES

C J Hobbs

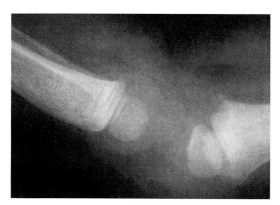

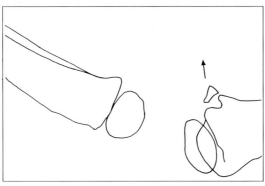

Metaphysial (corner) fracture of lower end of femur in a child of 15 months who was swung by the legs and hit head against a wall

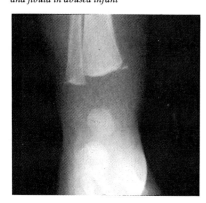

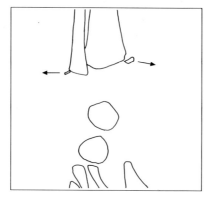

Distal metaphysial chip fractures of lower end of tibia and fibula in abused infant

Fractures are among the most serious injuries sustained after physical abuse. They may occur in almost any bone and may be single or multiple, clinically obvious or occult and detectable only by radiography.

Prevalence

In one study of physically abused children more than half of the children (58%) were under 3 years old and they sustained most of the fractures (94%). In contrast, accidental fractures occur more commonly in children of school age.

The proportion of children presenting to hospital with fractures resulting from physical abuse rises to a maximum during the first year of life, when it may be as high as a half. A great deal of suspicion is required at this age. Most accidental fractures in infants and toddlers result from falls, although fractures are uncommon in falls of under a metre.

As early detection improves the proportion of children with fractures who are identified as having been physically abused falls from 50% to 10% or less. Most children with serious injury have suffered minor injury or shown other signs of abuse that have not been recognised or acted on by professionals in contact with the child.

Detecting fractures due to physical abuse

Children whose fractures are the result of an accident present crying excessively, with swelling or bruising, and are reluctant to use the affected part—for example, to put weight on a leg.

Some fractures caused by physical abuse are detected only by radiology because the fracture may be old, the physical signs having regressed; the site may be hidden—for example, the ribs, pelvis, or skull—and the parents will not have drawn attention to the possibility of injury.

Important patterns

Six important patterns are seen in fractures caused by physical abuse. These are (*a*) a single fracture with multiple bruises; (*b*) multiple fractures in different stages of healing, possibly with no bruises or soft tissue injuries; (*c*) metaphysial-epiphysial injuries, which are often multiple; (*d*) rib fractures; (*e*) the formation of new periosteal bone; and (*f*) a skull fracture in association with intracranial injury.

As with all forms of physical abuse a careful history and examination and appraisal of the

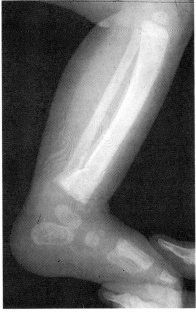
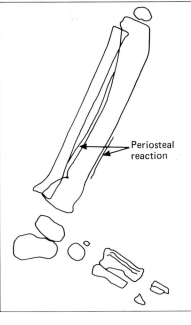

Periosteal reaction

Distal non-displaced fracture of lower shafts of tibia and fibula in abused child of 6 months, with evidence of periosteal reaction along tibial shafts. Fracture is probably 10-14 days old. Other injuries included multiple rib and complex skull fractures

fractures are specific for physical abuse in young children.

Cardiopulmonary resuscitation does not cause rib fractures in this age group.

Rib fractures are often multiple and bilateral and occur posteriorly. They are caused by thoracic compression, which often occurs with shaking and from kicks or blows in older children. Recent fractures are difficult to see but are more obvious later when callus forms as beaded shafts after about 10-14 days.

family potential for child abuse provides the framework for diagnosis.

Skeletal survey

The radiographic survey of the child's skeleton must be complete. Babygrams (the whole baby in one radiograph) are generally unacceptable.

Consider skeletal survey

- When injury or history suggest physical abuse
- In all children less than 18 months old
- In older children with severe bruising
- For localised pain, limp, or reluctance to use arm or leg
- When history of skeletal injury present
- In children dying in unusual or suspicious circumstances.

Specificity of radiological findings

No lesion is absolutely pathognomonic of physical abuse but some carry higher specificity than others.

High specificity findings are metaphysial or epiphysial fractures, or both (corner and bucket handle fractures, chip fractures); rib fractures; multiple or wide complex skull fractures, or both; scapular and sternal fractures, which are uncommon; multiple fractures; fractures of different ages; and unpresented fractures.

Low specificity findings are single fractures; linear, narrow parietal skull fractures; fractures in the shafts of long bones; and clavicular fractures.

Rib fractures

Rib fractures are usually occult and detected only by careful radiology, unless there is a history of direct trauma to the rib cage—for example, a road traffic accident—or bone disease. Rib

Metaphysial and epiphysial fractures

Metaphysial and epiphysial fractures are the classic injuries of physical abuse. Fragments of bone become separated from the ends of long bones either as a chip or as a whole plate. Such injuries arise from acceleration and deceleration as the infant is shaken by the body, arms, or legs. The forces of pulling and twisting applied to the weak metaphysial areas of bone disrupt a fine layer of new trabecular bone close to the junction with cartilage. In epiphysial lesions the injury occurs in the zone of hypertrophic cartilage with few radiological signs initially. The usual sites are the knee, wrist, elbow, and ankle.

Fractures of the shafts of long bones

Spiral, oblique, or transverse fractures arise in the shafts of long bones from indirect trauma—

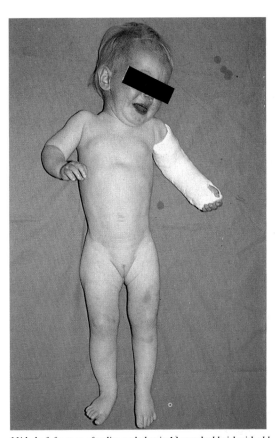

Mid-shaft fracture of radius and ulna in 14 month old girl with old bruising to her thigh and failure to thrive. Fracture in itself carries little specificity for physical abuse, but bruising and growth chart (overleaf) greatly increase likelihood of physical abuse.
Cohabiting boyfriend of girl's mother admitted swinging child by arm

Fractures

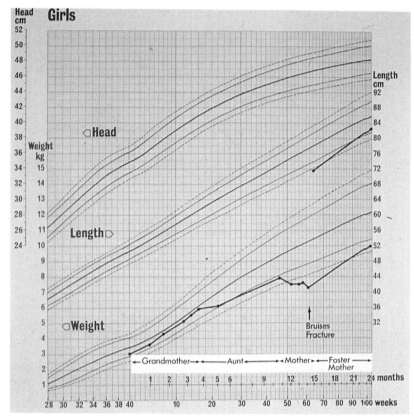

Growth chart of 14 month old girl with fractured tibia and fibula in case described on previous page. Pattern of failure to thrive developed from age of 4 months, when care was transferred to an aunt, and worsened when natural mother took over care at about 12 months. Catch up in length and weight were seen in foster mother's care. Children may react to changes in carer by developing behavioural difficulties, often centred on feeding, which may trigger violent responses from parents

for example, being swung by the arms—or direct trauma—for example, being hit across straightened arms with an iron bar, which causes symmetrical transverse fractures of the lower third of both radii.

Spiral fracture of the humerus was found to be significantly more common in physical abuse than in accidents in one study, but all types of fractures can arise from either physical abuse or an accident. Only the history or presence of other injuries will help differentiate between the two.

Posterior healing rib fractures of left sixth, seventh, and eighth ribs behind cardiac shadow in abused infant. Presence of callus and unclear fracture line suggests fractures are at least two weeks old

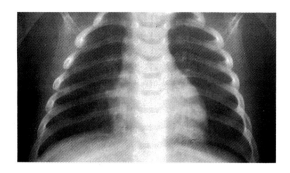

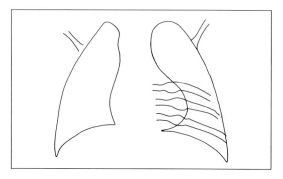

Spinal injury

Spinal injury in physical abuse usually results from hyperflexion-extension injury with damage to several consecutive levels. Defects in the lucency of the anterior superior edges of the vertebral bodies, often in the lower thoracic and upper lumbar regions, with narrowed disc spaces are characteristic. Multiple spinous process fractures are also described. Spinal cord injury may follow dislocation or subluxation.

Formation of new periosteal bone

Injury to an infant's developing long bone often results in subperiosteal haemorrhage, which raises the periosteum from the shaft while maintaining its firm attachment to the epiphysis. This process usually takes 10-14 days to appear, and radiography may yield negative results initially. The finding may also point to an underlying fracture that is not easily visualised.

Such injuries probably arise when arms and legs are grabbed, pulled, or used as a handle for shaking the child. Trauma must be distinguished from other causes—namely, infection, Caffey's disease, vitamin A intoxication, leukaemia, and certain drugs—but all of these are far less common than physical abuse.

Dating fractures

The dating of fractures is of obvious medicolegal importance. Fractures heal in distinct stages, which can be detected radiographically, according to a set time scale, shown in the table. The table gives peak times; sometimes the earliest changes are seen a few days before this.

Resolution of soft tissue change	4-10 days
Periosteal new bone formation (earliest sign)	10-14 days
Loss of fracture line definition	14-21 days
Soft callus	14-21 days
Hard callus	21-42 days
Remodelling	1 year

From: Kleinman PK. *Diagnostic imaging of child abuse.* Baltimore: Williams and Wilkins, 1987.

Repetitive injury to fractures that have not been medically treated may prolong the healing stages. Infants tend to heal more quickly than older children. Refracture through an old untreated fracture can be recognised by the presence of well developed callus around a fresh fracture with a clearly visible fracture line.

Differential diagnosis of fractures

Child abuse is common. Non-traumatic causes of fracture or pseudofracture vary from uncommon to extremely rare. A balanced perspective is required if children's interests are to be preserved. Courts for the protection of

Distal humerus epiphysial separation in 5 month old infant with 25 separate non-accidental injuries, including five fractures. Initially injury was confused with dislocation but on follow up four weeks later extensive formation of medial new bone (right) confirmed displacement of epiphysis

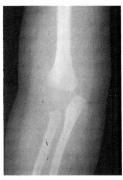 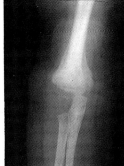 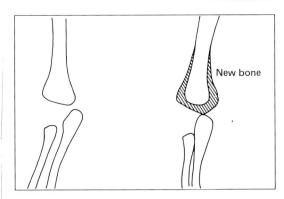

New bone

Spinal injury in abused 6 year old child. Characteristic injury is present

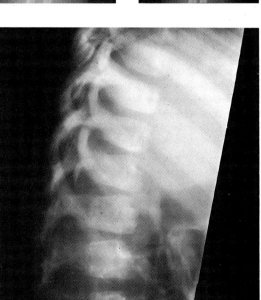 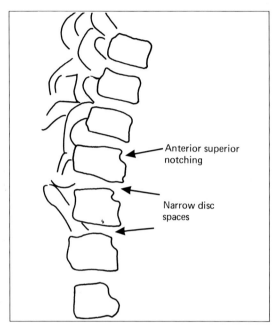

Anterior superior notching

Narrow disc spaces

children require probability rather than certainty in evidence.

Normal variants—The formation of new periosteal bone in infants and unusual suture lines in a skull radiograph could be normal variants.

Birth trauma—During breech deliveries the clavicle and humerus are often broken. If, however, callus is absent two weeks after birth the fracture did not occur during delivery.

Bone disease—Osteogenesis imperfecta, rickets of prematurity, disuse osteoporosis, copper deficiency, Caffey's disease, and osteomyelitis can cause fractures and need to be excluded. Features in the history and examination, however, help to exclude these uncommon conditions. Expert radiological, paediatric, and biochemical help may be needed in occasional

cases. The presence of a normal skeleton radiologically is strongly against the diagnosis of genetic, metabolic, or bone disease. In Leeds over 10 years fewer than five cases of physical abuse have been confused with bone disease.

I thank Dr M F G Buchanan for his help and the staff of the Department of Medical Illustration, St James's University Hospital, Leeds, for their help with the illustrations.

Further reading

Kleinman PK. *Diagnostic imaging of child abuse.* Baltimore: Williams and Wilkins, 1987.
Kempe CH, Silverman FN, Steele BF, Droegemueller W, Silver HK. The battered child syndrome. *JAMA* 1962;**181**:17-24.
Buchanan MFG. The recognition of non-accidental injury in children. *Practitioner* 1985;**229**:815-9.
Silverman FN. Radiology and other imaging procedures. In: Helfer RE, Kempe RS, eds. *The battered child.* 4th ed. Chicago: University of Chicago Press, 1987:214.
Warlock P, Stower M, Barbor P. Patterns of fractures in accidental and non-accidental injury in children: a comparative study. *Br Med J* 1986;**293**:100-2.

HEAD INJURIES

C J Hobbs

Head injuries, with or without fracture of the skull, are the commonest cause of death from battering, but abdominal injury to the gut or solid organs can mimic the signs of head injury and can lead to death if they are unrecognised.

Over 95% of serious intracranial injuries during the first year of life are the result of physical abuse.

Head injuries after abuse include skull fractures, subdural haematomas, subarachnoid haemorrhages, scalp bruises, traumatic alopecia, and subgaleal haematomas. In addition, between 40% and 70% of battered children have some sort of injury to the face or head, of which bruising is the most common.

Detecting head injuries due to physical abuse

When an infant rolls off a changing table, hospital trolley, cot, or bed, even on to a hard floor, serious injury rarely occurs. In one study 80% of infants escaped without any findings of injury whatsoever. The other 20% had a single cut, lump, or bruise. Skull fractures were found in 1%, and these were single and linear. An equal number had a fracture at another site, of which the clavicle and humerus were the most common. No child sustained a subdural haematoma or life threatening condition. Falls from greater heights (between 1 and 2 m), as, for example, from a standing adult's shoulder, are more likely to result in a single linear parietal hairline fracture of

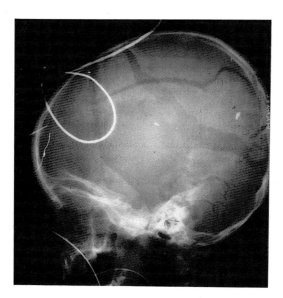
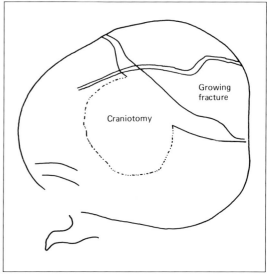

Extensive bilateral parietal fractures, which are wide and growing. Large lucent area represents surgical evacuation of large haematoma before 15 month old child died. Head was injured when the child was swung by the leg against a wall

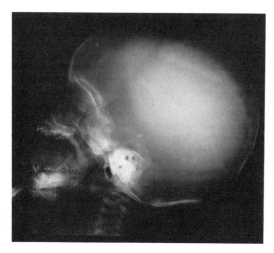
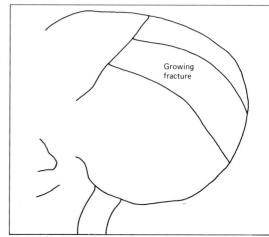

Growing fracture of parietal bone in 6 week old abused child. Father claimed to have dropped child, but old rib fractures and intracranial injury were inconsistent with history

Manifestations of skull fractures

Child usually said to have fallen or banged head—for example, on door—or history may be absent

	Accident	Physical abuse
Type	Single linear	Multiple, complex, branched
Maximum fracture width	Hairline, narrow, 1-2 mm	Wide, growing, 3 mm or more
Site	Parietal One bone only	Occipital, highly specific Bilateral, parietal More than one bone affected
Depressed	Localised with clear history of fall on to sharp object	As part of complex fracture, extensive or multiple depressed areas
Associated intracranial injury	Unusual except after severe falls (2-3 m or more). Extradural haemorrhage uncommon but serious complication of simple fracture	Subdural haemorrhage, cerebral contusion, intracerebral haemorrhage, and cerebral oedema common

If an infant presents with a cranial swelling a day or two after a minor head injury and has a hairline parietal single linear fracture the cause is usually innocent provided that other injuries are not present

scaling, which helps differentiate it from other forms of alopecia.

Skull fractures

Fractures indicate blunt impact injuries. Their reliable detection in a radiograph requires a radiologist or doctor experienced in differentiating usual and unusual suture lines in infants, which may be difficult. Swelling over the area helps, but the radiograph needs to be examined with bright light illumination.

The radiograph must be interpreted alongside the history. When there is a history of a minor fall, as is usually the case in infants and toddlers during the first two years, significant differences exist between the patterns of fracture after abuse and those after an accident. These are summarised in the table.

After abuse fractures tend to be extensive, multiple, complex or branched, depressed, wide, separated, and growing and to cross individual suture lines, thereby affecting many individual skull bones. Whereas in accidents the parietal bone alone is usually affected by a single narrow linear fracture, in abuse other bones, notably the thick occipital bone and the base of the skull, are more likely to be fractured. Indeed, a fracture of the occipital bone should carry a high suspicion of abuse.

Growing fractures are not generally well known among doctors. These uncommon fractures occur only in infancy and entail a dural tear and brain injury beneath the fracture, which subsequently enlarges to form a cranial defect. Once a fracture reaches 0·5 cm in width in a radiograph it should be carefully followed for further growth. Such fractures seem to occur after a more severe blow to the head and are therefore more likely to be associated with abuse. Surgical treatment may be required to repair the defect.

the skull, and the infant may be irritable, vomit, or refuse a feed. Serious intracranial injury is extremely unlikely.

Even in more serious falls from heights in excess of 2 m or down stairs where a fracture may show one or two features of abuse (table), serious intracranial injury is unusual. Occasionally, however, extradural haemorrhage can, if unrecognised and untreated, be fatal irrespective of the presence or absence of an underlying cerebral injury.

The force entailed in physical abuse—for example, in swinging the child, in violent uncontrolled shaking, and in hitting the child's head with a fist or foot or against a wall—is so much greater that the pattern of injury is different and serious intracranial injury results. Accidental intracranial injury in infancy is rare.

Scalp injury

The presence of injury to the scalp is often shown by a swelling, which can reach considerable size. This may represent bruising to the scalp tissues; if there is a fracture a subgaleal haematoma forms, into which much blood may be lost. Subgaleal haematoma also results from hair pulling as, for example, when a child is picked up by the hair. The swelling is diffuse and boggy and there are broken hairs with occasionally petechiae at the roots. There are no signs of scalp disease, such as loose hairs or

Subdural haematoma

Subdural haematomas arise in over half of cases without the presence of a skull fracture. For a while they were termed "spontaneous subdural haematomas" until it was recognised that the infants had been abused. The evidence points to violent shaking disrupting bridging cerebral veins with bleeding into the subdural space, often over a wide area bilaterally.

In some cases the only additional evidence is the presence of retinal haemorrhages and there may be no bruising or other injury to the baby. These babies have been shaken violently, usually to stop them crying. Bouncing a baby up and down on a knee or an accidental head injury resulting in a simple fracture does not result in subdural haematomas.

Subdural haematomas arising after birth trauma produce signs and symptoms soon after delivery and should not lead to confusion. The concept of a chronic subdural haematoma after birth trauma is extremely dubious.

Head injuries

Retinal haemorrhage in abused child

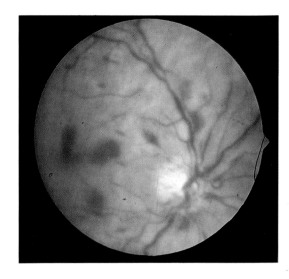

Subdural haematoma

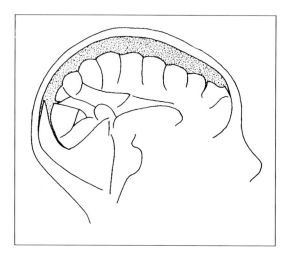

Children who develop irritability, vomiting, decreasing levels of consciousness, and irregular breathing or apnoea shortly after an alleged trivial head injury have probably been abused. Parents may admit to mildly shaking the child because "he didn't look too good" or "stopped breathing." In reality the child has been violently shaken. The diagnosis, once thought of, is most easily confirmed by computed tomography, but this can occasionally miss a difficult case.

Retinal haemorrhages

Like subdural haematoma, with which retinal haemorrhages often coexist, the presence of retinal haemorrhages without adequate explanation is strong presumptive evidence of child abuse. Whiplash injury from shaking leads to a short term rise in intracranial pressure, which leads to increased pressure in the central retinal vein with consequent retinal haemorrhage. Pupils should be dilated with a mydriatic such as 1% cyclopentolate drops and the fundi examined. This may be easier when the baby is feeding or sucking. Retinal haemorrhages in newborn infants after a difficult delivery disappear during the first days of life.

Cerebral contusion, haemorrhage, and oedema

Cerebral contusion, haemorrhage, and oedema are responsible for many of the deaths and long term disability resulting from physical abuse. Areas of cerebral disruption, haemorrhage, and oedema are scattered throughout the brain, which swells, leading to a short term rise in intracranial pressure. Surgery is rarely helpful.

If the child survives chronic disability is a real possibility. In one study Buchanan and Oliver estimated that between 3% and 11% of children residing in hospitals for the retarded were handicapped as a result of violent abuse. They described seizures and post-traumatic hydrocephalus, damage to visual pathways, and cerebral infarction leading to atrophy and microcephaly.

"Non-traumatic" presentation of abusive head injuries

There may be no history of trauma or obvious signs of injury in a child with a head injury caused by physical abuse. Unexplained neurological deficit, seizures, apnoeic attacks, hydrocephalus, and raised intracranial pressure may be occult manifestations of child abuse. Trauma should also be considered along with meningitis and encephalitis, tumours, spontaneous intracranial haemorrhage, non-traumatic hydrocephalus, and administration of drugs and poisons. A radiograph of the skull, a skeletal survey, lumbar puncture, careful examination of the fundi, and computed tomography are helpful in diagnosis.

I thank Dr M F G Buchanan for his help, and the staff of the Department of Medical Illustration, St James's University Hospital, Leeds, for their help with the illustrations.

Further reading

Guthkelch AN. Infantile subdural haematoma and its relationship to whiplash injuries. *Br Med J* 1971;ii:430-1.
Billmire ME, Myers PA. Serious head injury in infants: accident or abuse? *Pediatrics* 1985;75:340-2.
Hobbs CJ. Skull fracture and the diagnosis of abuse. *Arch Dis Child* 1984;59:246-52.
Helfer RE, Slovis TL, Black M. Injuries resulting when small children fall out of bed. *Pediatrics* 1977;60:533-5.
Caffey J. Multiple fractures in the long bone of infants suffering from chronic subdural haematoma. *American Journal of Roentgenology* 1946; 56:163–73.

BURNS AND SCALDS

C J Hobbs

Accident	— lapse in usual protection given to the child
Neglect	— inadequate or negligent parenting, failing to protect the child
Abuse	— deliberately inflicted injury

Accidental burns and scalds in children occur because of a lapse in the usual protection given to the child. Neglected children may be burnt because of inadequate or negligent parenting, which is a failure to protect the child, whereas in abused children burns and scalds are deliberately inflicted.

Burns and scalds within the range of child abuse are seen as serious injuries, as sadistic and linked with the sexual or violent arousal of an adult, and as punitive to evoke fear ("I'll teach him a lesson").

Prevalence

Deliberately inflicted burns and scalds are found in 10% of physically abused children, 5% of sexually abused children, and 1-16% of all children presenting at hospital with burns and scalds. This form of physical abuse is, however,

underrecognised and underreported because diagnosis may be difficult.

The peak age of children accidentally burning or scalding themselves is during the second year; the peak age of children being deliberately burnt is during the third year.

Types of thermal injury

Scalds—These are caused by hot water—for example, in drinks, liquid food, and baths. Scalds cause blisters and the affected skin peels in sheets and is soggy and blanched. They have a characteristic shape: they follow the contours of clothes and are enhanced by them, and drip, pour, and splash patterns are seen. The depth of injury is variable and contoured.

Contact, dry burns—Such burns are caused by hot objects, usually metallic, and electric fires. The injury looks like a brand mark, sharply demarcated and with the shape of the object that caused it. The burn is dry and tends to be of a uniform depth.

Burns from flames—These are caused by fires and matches and may be identified by charring and by singed hairs.

Cigarette burns—These leave a circular mark and a tail if the cigarette was brushed against the skin. In physical abuse the burn tends to form a crater and to scar because the injury is deep. The injury may be multiple but it is not particularly common.

Electrical burns—These are small but deep with exit and entry points.

Friction burns—These occur when, for example, a child is dragged across a floor. Bony prominences are affected and the blisters are broken.

Chemical burns—These may cause staining and scarring of the skin.

Radiant burns—These are caused by radiant energy—for example, from a fire or the sun. Injury is usually extensive and affects one aspect of an arm or leg or the body and is limited by clothing. The skin shows erythema and blistering. Such burns occur in children who are made to stand in front of a fire.

Depth of burns and scalds

The depth of burns depends on the temperature and time of exposure. At 44°C it takes 6-7 hours for full thickness destruction of the skin, at 70°C only 1 second, and at 60°C (the temperature of the hot water supply in many homes) about 10 seconds.

The other factor determining the depth of

Left: Contact burns in 2 year old boy with developmental retardation who was abused by his mother. Burns to penis were also present. Right: End of curtain wire heated in fire that was responsible for burns

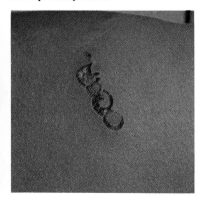

Cratered deep cigarette burn in typical site on back of hand in 5 year old boy, who also said, "Mummy put her fingers in my bottom"

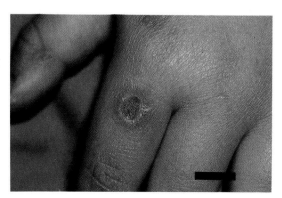

Burns and scalds

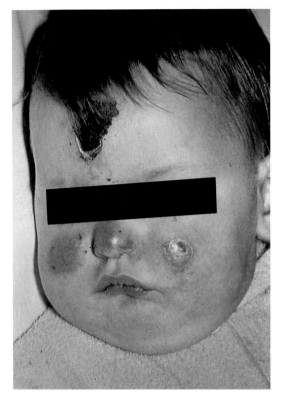

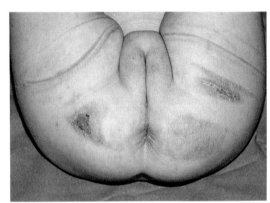

injury is the thickness of the skin. The above figures relate to adults and guinea pigs, and the time for children, particularly infants, is probably less. Deep burns leave permanent scars, which can provide later evidence of physical abuse.

History of physical abuse

In physical abuse the history of the burn is not consistent with the injury—for example, a two year old is said to have got into a bath of warm water, turned on the hot tap, and burnt both feet. There is a delay in seeking treatment or treatment is avoided altogether, the injury being discovered by chance.

The parent may deny that the injury is a burn when it clearly is and offer an unlikely explanation. The doctor may be told that the child did it to himself or that a sibling did. The incident is often unwitnessed ("I didn't see what happened, but he might have . . .") whereas in accidental injury to toddlers and young children parents are usually very clear what happened, even if they did not themselves see it.

A child who has been deliberately burnt may say that it did not hurt and the parent may tell the doctor that the child did not cry, which represents denial of what has happened. Alternatively, the child's history may disagree with that of the parents. The mother might say that the child fell over on to the fire and the child tell a nurse quietly, "Mummy did it."

In physical abuse repeated burns are seen. In accidents once is usually enough for most parents and children.

Important sites and patterns
Accidental burns

Most common scalds in toddlers and older infants occur when the child pulls kettles, pans, or cups of hot water or drinks from a kitchen unit or table. The scald affects the face, shoulders, upper arms, and upper trunk.

Accidental scalding from hot baths leaves an irregular mark with splashes.

Contact burns tend to be superficial, except in accidents with electric bar fires in which the hand

Left: Scalds from coffee thrown by drunken father at 3 year old girl producing scattered splash effect. Differentiation from accidental scalds from pouring liquids may be difficult

Right: Accidental scald typical of child pulling kettle from work surface by flex. Burn is variable thickness and head and shoulders take brunt of injury

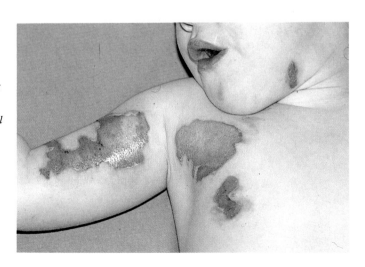

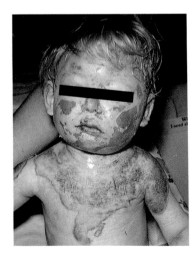

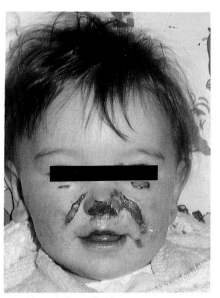

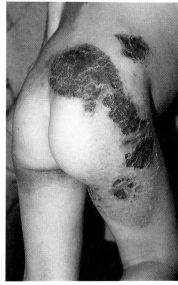

sticks to the bar and sustains deep destructive burns to the palm.

Burns due to physical abuse

Non-accidental burns affect the face and head, perineum, buttocks and genitalia, the hands, and the feet and legs.

Cigarette burns may be seen on the face and head. Burns may be seen around rather than in the mouth when food has been pushed into the face.

To punish wetting and soiling misdemeanours or cure problems with wetting, abusing parents may dip the child's buttocks into a bath of hot water. The centre of the burn may show sparing where the buttocks pressed on to the bath—the so called "hole in the doughnut" effect. Burns to the perineum and genitalia may be part of sexual abuse.

Hands commonly show burns to the dorsal surface in physical abuse, whereas in accidents—for example, with an electric fire—the palm is affected. Hands are burnt by being held under a tap or on to hot objects.

The soles of the feet may show contact or cigarette burns. Burns on the feet and ankles may show a stocking or glove distribution with no splash marks and a clear tide mark when they have been caused by forced immersion in a sink or bath. Contact burns from fires (grid marks), irons, and curling tongs may also be seen on the legs and feet.

Food burns in 9 month old child with failure to thrive that allegedly occurred when he was left alone with bowl of hot food. Parents' refusal to allow admission to hospital, absence of burns in mouth, and failure to match burn with supplied utensil left serious doubts

Extensive bath scalds in 3 year old girl failing to thrive. Central part of buttock spared where pressed on to cool base of bath—"hole in doughnut" effect. Abuse suspected but unproved

Admitted abuse in boy aged 3 years. Hand was held under hot tap

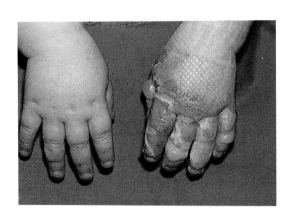

Characteristics of parents and children

Parents may be hostile, abusive to staff, and angry. They may refuse to allow the child to be admitted despite the need for treatment or threaten to discharge the child prematurely. Mothers who burn their children may be depressed, withdrawn, seeking help, and be themselves victims of child abuse (often sexual abuse).

In contrast to parents of accidentally burnt children abusing parents may show a lack of concern for the child or a lack of guilt. Parents of accidentally burnt children are often defensive, guilty, and dislike being questioned about the

Boy aged 30 months with symmetrical stocking scalds (full thickness in part) to both feet and superficial scald to buttock with unaffected intervening areas. History of unwitnessed bathing accident but forced immersion later admitted

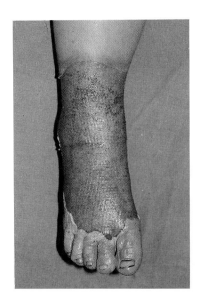

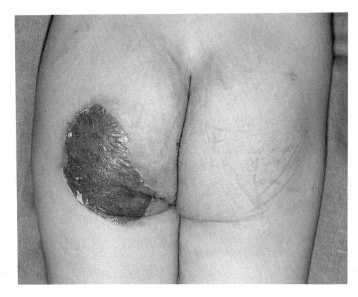

cause of the injury, which should not be misinterpreted as evidence of physical abuse.

A disturbed interaction between parent and child may show itself as anger and hostility towards the child—"It's his fault"—or as disregard of or an inability to cope with the child's behaviour. Abused children may be excessively withdrawn, passive, and uncomplaining about dressings or extremely anxious, hyperactive, angry, and rebellious, especially in the children's ward. In older children a reluctance to talk about their injury and how it occurred is worrying.

Assessment

Assessment is multidisciplinary and entails the participation of doctors (general practitioner, accident and emergency doctor, plastic surgeon, and consultant paediatrician), nurses, health visitors, social workers, police officers, and forensic scientists. In other words, the social services, the primary health care team, the hospital team, and the police need to liaise.

Visits to the child's home with the police may be required to inspect the bathroom, kitchen, fires, and household equipment.

History—This must be detailed and give the exact time of the incident, the sequence of events, and the action taken. Is the child's developmental ability consistent with what he is said to have done? For example, could an 18 month old child climb into a bath in the way stated?

Examination—Draw, measure, and photograph the injury. Manipulate the child's posture to discover his position when the injury occurred. Record the depth of the injury in relation to the temperature. Look for other injuries and look for signs of sexual abuse during genital and anal examinations. Assess the child's demeanour, behaviour, and development. In physical abuse a failure to thrive and a delay in acquiring language are common. Finally, always ask the child what happened.

Differential diagnosis

When there is a lesion and no history of a burn skin infection or disease should be considered. Examples of conditions that may mimic burns are epidermolysis bullosa, impetigo, papular urticaria, contact dermatitis, and severe nappy rash.

Improbable accidents can occur. For example, a child could be burnt by vinegar, as concentrated vinegar (glacial acetic acid) has a pH of 1·6. In addition, the buckles of seat belts or black vinyl seats heated by the sun have caused injuries that have been confused with physical abuse. In general central heating radiators are safe but hands have been badly burnt when they have been trapped behind one, and the injudicious use of hot water bottles for babies has resulted in burns that are caused by neglect rather than abuse.

Anaesthesia, an inability to move, or neurological deficit caused by a congenital insensitivity to pain, syringomyelia, spina bifida, mental disability, cerebral palsy, and epilepsy may be associated with unusual burns and scalds.

Neglect should also be considered. Children left alone at home have an increased risk of dying in house fires. Fireguards are required by law for children under 12. Negligent parents may fail to seek treatment when their children are burnt. Therefore the effects of neglect are serious and should also be reported to protective agencies.

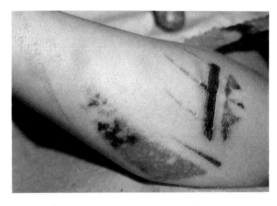

Inflicted contact burn on gas fire in 4 year old boy. Mother said dog knocked him on to fire when she was out of room. Child said that his mother did it. Burn was old and healing and was not presented for treatment. Child kept away from school

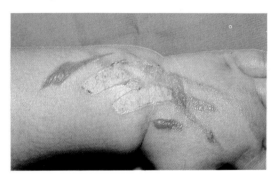

Partial thickness grid burn on back of wrist of 11 month old baby allegedly caused by older sibling. Mother later admitted responsibility for this single injury

Further reading

Hight DW, Bakalar HR, Lloyd J. Inflicted burns in children. Recognition and treatment. *JAMA* 1979;**242**:517-20.

Keen JH, Lendrum J, Wolman B. Inflicted burns and scalds in children. *Br Med J* 1975;iv:268-9.

Hobbs CJ. When are burns not accidental? *Arch Dis Child* 1986;**61**:357-61.

Lenoski EF, Hunter KA. Specific patterns of inflicted burn injuries. *J Trauma* 1977;**17**:842.

Feldman KW. Child abuse by burning. In: Helfer RE, Kempe RS, eds. *The battered child*. 4th ed. Chicago: Chicago University Press, 1987:197.

POISONING

Roy Meadow

A three year old child presented with recurrent bouts of drowsiness. At first the mother denied giving drugs inappropriately but subsequently displayed them together with the container in which she kept them

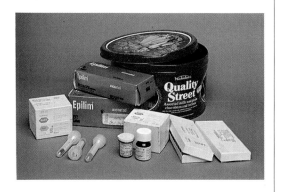

Accidental poisoning is very common; non-accidental poisoning is uncommon but more serious. Accidental poisoning commonly occurs in toddlers aged 2 to 4 who explore the world with their mouth and try out any medicines, tablets, or other liquids that they find. The parent finds the 3 year old with an empty bottle in the bathroom or kitchen and is unsure how much the child has ingested. Usually the child has swallowed little or nothing and it is a poisoning scare rather than a true poisoning event. Less than 15% of the thousands of children presenting to hospital because of accidental poisoning develop symptoms from the drug; death is extremely rare. Death from non-accidental poisoning is more common.

It is important to be aware that sometimes the parent will have poisoned the child. Therefore the story must always be checked to make sure that it makes sense—could that young a child have had access to those particular tablets? (2 year old children probably cannot reach the top shelf of the kitchen cupboard, neither can they easily unwrap individually foil packed tablets or open a child resistant container. Child resistant containers are not childproof, but they do delay the child's access to the contents).

Detecting non-accidental poisoning

Deliberate poisoning mainly occurs in children below the age of 2½ years. Children who have been poisoned by a parent are likely to present in four main ways.

(1) The child presents as a poisoning scare in which the parent rushes the child to hospital claiming that the child has ingested the drug accidentally.

(2) The child presents with inexplicable symptoms and signs, usually of acute onset. These are summarised in the table together with some of the drugs that have been given intentionally by parents to children.

(3) The child presents with recurrent unexplained illnesses that have the features in the table—for example, recurrent episodes of drowsiness or hyperventilation. These sorts of patients overlap with those for whom parents create false illness (Munchausen syndrome by proxy) by other means.

(4) The child may be moribund or dead when first seen by the doctor.

In all cases check for other forms of abuse and for sudden unexplained deaths in other members of the family.

Motive

The motive for poisoning varies and includes parents who are vindictive and seeking to teach their child a lesson, parents who are themselves addicted to drugs such as methadone or cannabis and involve the child from an early age, and parents who seek to make a healthy child seem to have a chronic illness.

Establishing poisoning

Identifying poisoning can be very difficult even when the doctor is alert to the possibility. Most hospitals have a limited biochemical screen confined to major common drugs for both blood and urine samples, but there is no fully comprehensive toxicology screen available. Therefore the doctor's job is, firstly, to think of possible drugs responsible for the child's symptoms, secondly, to try to identify from the

One of the commonest poisons given by parents is table salt, sodium chloride. Usually a child will excrete excess salt speedily in the urine but if deprived of water will be unable to do so. Then hypernatraemia develops causing initial thirst and irritation followed by drowsiness and seizures. Death occurs in extreme cases. The high serum sodium concentration will be associated with an extremely high sodium concentration in the urine.

Symptoms and signs	Drug
Seizures and apnoeic spells	Salt (sodium chloride)
	Phenothiazines
	Tricyclic antidepressants
	Hydrocarbons
Hyperventilation	Salicylates
	Acids
Drowsiness and stupor	Hypnotics
	Insulin
	Aspirin
	Paracetamol
	Tricyclic antidepressants
	Anticonvulsants
	Phenothiazines
	Methadone
	Cannabis
Hallucinations	Atropine-like agents
Bizarre motor movements (myoclonic jerks, tremors, extrapyramidal signs)	Phenothiazines
	Metoclopramide
	Antihistamines
Vomiting	Emetics and many other drugs
Diarrhoea (with or without failure to thrive)	Laxatives, including magnesium hydroxide (Milk of Magnesia) and phenolphthalein
	Salt
Haematemesis	Salicylates
	Iron
Ulcerated mouth	Corrosives
Thirst	Salt (with or without water deprivation)
Bizarre biochemical blood profile	Salt
	Insulin
	Salicylates
	Sodium bicarbonate

general practitioner or hospital records any drugs that might be present in that household or to which the mother has access, and then, thirdly, to ask the laboratory to look specifically for that drug in the child's blood. It is worth finding out if the parents' jobs give them access to particular drugs—for example, if a parent is a nurse or works in a hospital. Until such information is available samples of blood, urine, and vomit, if available, should be kept safely in the refrigerator. A few drugs are radio-opaque so that a straight abdominal radiograph may be helpful if taken within a few hours of ingestion.

It is particularly important to preserve samples of blood, urine, and tissues when a child is brought in moribund with apparent encephalopathy, liver failure, bleeding disorder, or bizarre biochemical results. When such children die it is mandatory to inform the coroner. Whenever there is a strong suspicion of poisoning the police should be informed; their regional forensic laboratories can be extremely helpful in analysing samples for they have one of the more detailed screening systems, but even these regional laboratories cannot screen for everything and they do their job best if they are given some idea of the type of drug to look for.

It is more important in the first place to try to identify the drug than the method by which the parent has given the drug to the child. Sometimes the methods are so bizarre that they defy the commonsense reasoning of a normal person. You just have to accept that parents do incredible things and that a determined parent can find ways of poisoning a child, even when under the closest supervision. Mothers have injected insulin into intravenous lines, poured medicine into a gastrostomy tube, put nasogastric tubes down into the child's stomach to administer particularly noxious solutions that the child would otherwise not take, secreted tablets in their mouth that they have passed on to the child with a kiss, and secreted drugs behind the glass eyeball of the teddy bear they have given to the child. The essential first step is to identify the poison and only then to start puzzling about how the child was given it.

If poisoning is suspected every chance should be given to the parent to explain how the child came to be given the poison. Many parents give drugs, tonics, and folk remedies to their child without telling doctors. Some are fearful of discussing it because they think the doctor would disapprove; others are embarrassed by trying a rather naive remedy for their child. Therefore the doctor should sympathetically explore with the parent the ways in which a child might have ingested a particular poison. This is particularly important for people from unconventional backgrounds or from different ethnic cultures, who may use many different sources of health advice apart from the NHS.

Poison centres

Poison centres provide good advice about the constituents of many proprietary and household products and also about treatment. They may also be helpful when you are faced with a child who has possibly been poisoned by suggesting ways of identifying the drug.

Poison information services
Belfast, 0232 240503
Birmingham, 021 554 3801
Cardiff, 0222 709901
Dublin, 0001 379964
Edinburgh, 031 229 2477
Leeds, 0532 430175
London, 01 635 9191
Newcastle 091 2325131

There are six regional forensic laboratories in England and Wales, each of which serves six or more police forces, and the London Metropolitan Police has its own laboratory. In general their work comes directly from the police, though some will accept work from doctors through the local Home Office pathologist. (The name and address of the Home Office pathologist can be obtained from the local coroner's office.)

Further reading
Rogers D, Tripp J, Bentovim A, Robinson A, Berry D, Goulding R. Non-accidental poisoning: an extended syndrome of child abuse. Br Med J 1976; i:793-6.

SUFFOCATION

Roy Meadow

The tyrannous and bloody act is done;
The most arch deed of piteous massacre
That ever yet this land was guilty of . . . .
. . . we smothered the most replenished
sweet work of nature . . .

> Sir James Tyrrell after the murder of the two
> child princes in the tower.
> SHAKESPEARE, *Richard III*

Asphyxia is an uncommon but serious form of child abuse. The commonest form is smothering and the abuser is usually the child's mother, who uses her hand, a pad of rolled up clothing, or a pillow to cause mechanical obstruction to the child's airways. Less commonly she presses the child's face against her chest, encloses the child's head in a plastic bag, or strangles by pressure on the child's neck.

Clinical features

Smothering happens to young children under the age of 3 years, most being infants under the age of 1 year. They may present to doctors either as sudden unexplained deaths ("cot deaths"), moribund "near miss cot deaths," or repetitively as cyanotic or floppy children whom the mother alleges to have had an episode at home—which is presumed by doctors to have been an apnoeic attack or a seizure. (If a mother describes a young baby as having stopped breathing or having seemed unconscious for a short time a doctor will probably consider that the baby has had an apnoeic attack, whereas in an older child he or she is more likely to consider the same description to have been a seizure.)

A small proportion of babies currently certified as having died from "the sudden infant death syndrome" have been killed by their parent. It is important to recognise this, but not to overemphasise it—for over 90% of parents who suffer the sudden death of their infant are blameless. The proportion of sudden infant deaths caused by a parent is uncertain and will vary from year to year and from country to country. The sort of psychosocial investigation required to identify such deaths is difficult to pursue and has been completed in only a few studies. Emery concludes, from his own and the work of others, that the proportion is less than one in 10 but more than one in 50. Smothering by the mother seems to be the usual mechanism. Some of the infants have had previous recurrent episodes of apnoea or seizures that may have been investigated thoroughly in a conventional radiological, biochemical, or electrophysiological way without proper consideration being given to child abuse as a possible cause. Warning features that the sudden infant death syndrome may have been caused by a mother smothering her child are:

● Previous episodes of unexplained apnoea, seizures, or "near miss cot death"
● An infant aged over 6 months
● Previous unexplained disorders affecting that child
● Other unexplained deaths of children in the same family.

For some children the smothering is associated with other forms of child abuse, particularly physical abuse and Munchausen syndrome by proxy.

Some mothers smother their child when they are feeling violent hatred towards their baby, others do it in a repetitive systematic way, taking their child regularly to the doctor each time that they have smothered their child for long enough to make him or her unconscious. For others it is an impulsive action at a time of frustration or stress at home.

And Then There Were None

During their 14 years as parents, Mary Beth and Joseph Tinning buried nine children. Until the last death, authorities never suspected wrongdoing. How could this happen?

THE GUARDIAN
Friday December 2 1988

First child 'smothered,' said mother

Upstate Mother Is Held

MOTHER accused of smothering the baby when murder of her second met her with a young man at hostel.

2-year-old had been hospitalized for what was called a fall down a flight of stairs. Social services

After 9 Babies Die in 14 Years, Mother Is Held

By AMY WALLACE
Special to The New York Times

It was not until Wednesday, when the police charged Mrs. Tinning, who is 43 old, with suffocating her

said there might have been incomplete examinations of the deaths and lapses communication among doc

Signs of smothering

Smothering is violent; a young child who cannot breathe struggles and tries to get air. The smothering needs considerable force, even when a child is young: the child has to be laid down on his back or against something firm for the mother to press hard on his face, alternatively the child is clutched closely into her chest. Despite the obvious violence entailed the signs may be very few. In general, someone who is asphyxiated tends to develop multiple petechiae on the face, particularly on the eyelids, as a result of the raised blood pressure, lack of oxygen, and retention of carbon dioxide. There may be congestive changes in the face too. Hand pressure on the face may leave thumbmarks or fingerprints around the nose or mouth or abrasions inside the mouth with bruising of the gums; but more often smothering is done with a pillow or with clothing and no external pressure marks are visible, and quite often neither petechiae nor swelling of the face are apparent. All forms of asphyxiation may be associated with some bleeding from the nose or mouth, but it is not inevitable. Thus a smothered infant may show no signs at all to the most experienced clinician or forensic pathologist. Although generally the smothering has to persist for a minute to cause seizures—longer to cause brain damage and perhaps two minutes (depending upon other circumstances) to cause death—damage may be more sudden and catastrophic if the child, as a result of the sudden assault, has a cardiac arrest or vomits and chokes.

Differential diagnosis

Unexplained episodes of apnoea or a seizure are commonly reported by mothers of young babies. Sometimes an anxious mother perceives illness that is not there or overinterprets the periodic breathing and normal movements of a healthy baby. Therefore in all such cases it is worth trying to get a description of the episodes from another relative. This is particularly important if the mother is suspected of causing the episodes.

True apnoea, in which the breathing stops for 20 seconds or more and is followed by bradycardia, cyanosis, or pallor, is frightening and often unexplained. It is more likely in small preterm babies and usually starts in the neonatal period. In early life both respiratory syncytial virus infection and whooping cough can be associated with spells of apnoea in previously well infants; the apnoea may precede the cough or other respiratory signs by a few days.

Whenever apnoea starts unexpectedly in a previously well baby it must be investigated thoroughly. The investigations should include careful checks for cardiac or respiratory disorder, oesophageal reflux, and a biochemical or seizure disorder. When these investigations give normal results consideration should be given to whether the episodes are being caused by the mother; if the episodes are frequent a period in hospital without the mother might be the wisest course. If the episodes are frequent when at home and absent when in hospital away from the mother, the mother is probably responsible—by acts of either omission or commission. Some hospital units are able to arrange video recording of the infant and mother in hospital. As a diagnostic test video surveillance is highly specific since filmed evidence of suffocation provides conclusive proof. But it is not very sensitive as most abuse occurs at home and even if the mother does suffocate her child in hospital she may well not do so during the period of video surveillance.

Sudden infant death syndrome (cot death)

The sudden infant death syndrome is the commonest category of death in Britain for infants aged between 1 month and 1 year. The label is given when no cause is found for the death of a previously well infant. Roughly two per 1000 live births are affected. It is commonest in the first five months of life and happens to previously well children who have not had episodes of apnoea or other unexplained illness. Recurrence within a family is extremely rare. The parents are not responsible or to blame for the tragic death of their child.

Further reading

Emery JL. Infanticide, filicide and cot death. *Arch Dis Child* 1985;**60**:505-7.
Light MJ, Sheridan MS. Munchausen syndrome by proxy and apnea. Presented at the fourth annual conference on infantile apnea and home monitoring of the high risk infant, Eisenhower Medical Center, Rancho, Mirage, California, January 1986.
Rosen CL, Frost JD Jr, Bricker T, Tarnow JD, Gillette PC, Dunlavy S. Two siblings with recurrent cardiorespiratory arrest: Munchausen syndrome by proxy or child abuse? *Pediatrics* 1983;**71**:715-20.
Southall DP, Stebbens VA, Rees SV, Lang MH, Warner JO, Shinebourne EA. Apnoeic episodes induced by smothering: two cases identified by covert video surveillance. *Br Med J* 1987;**294**:1637-41.

EMOTIONAL ABUSE AND NEGLECT

David H Skuse

Emotional abuse and neglect of children may take many forms from a lack of care for their physical needs, through a failure to provide consistent love and nurture, to overt hostility and rejection. Deleterious effects upon developing children are correspondingly diverse and tend to vary with age. In infancy neglect of physical care is likely to produce the most obvious consequences and developmental delays are also found. Preschool children may additionally present with disorders of social and emotional adjustment. Older children are likely to show behavioural problems at school, which are often accompanied by extensive learning difficulties. Emotional abuse is rarely the sole reason for seeking child protection through legal action, yet evidence is accumulating that its long term consequences upon social, emotional, and cognitive development may be far reaching and profound.

Defining features

Emotional abuse refers to the habitual verbal harassment of a child by disparagement, criticism, threat and ridicule, and the inversion of love; by verbal and non-verbal means rejection and withdrawal are substituted. Neglect comprises both a lack of physical caretaking and supervision and a failure to engage the developmental needs of the child in terms of cognitive stimulation. Although direct observation of parenting may raise suspicions about the presence of emotional abuse and neglect, the diagnosis is usually suggested by its consequences in the child: "the severe adverse

effect on the behaviour and emotional development of a child caused by persistent or severe emotional ill-treatment or rejection."[1] All abuse entails some emotional ill treatment. There is often accompanying physical or sexual abuse. Without signs of physical or sexual maltreatment and disclosure of specific abusive activities, however, it is still possible to recognise characteristic groups of features that demand further investigation. Current knowledge on the subject does not yet allow us causally to link specific patterns of maltreatment to particular delays and disorders. In addition, the symptoms and signs to be described are not invariably indicative of abuse and neglect. But the cessation of abuse and its substitution with sensitive care—often in an alternative home—is usually followed by a rapid and dramatic improvement in developmental attainments, behaviour, and socioemotional adjustment.

Infants

Neglect of the physical and emotional nurture of an infant is likely to result in various signs and symptoms that should be fairly easily recognised. The aspects of physical development that are affected are those that demand the closest attention from caregivers. Babies are dependent creatures: they need to be fed regularly, to be kept in a reasonably dry and warm environment, and to have their bowel and bladder functions taken care of. If they are habitually cold and wet they will contract recurrent infections; if they do not have their nappies changed regularly they will develop nappy rash, which if neglected may cause scarring; if they are not fed adequately they will fail to thrive. Failure to thrive is usually defined as an exceptionally poor rate of growth in which weight (and often length) becomes increasingly divergent from normal age standardised values in the population. There are many reasons why such a pattern of growth may occur. Recent population surveys show that it is only exceptionally associated with abuse or deliberate neglect—even in non-organic cases. In families in which abuse is suspected other evidence to support those suspicions should be sought.

When there has been serious neglect social and psychomotor skills are also likely to be affected. If there has been no encouragement to acquire skills such as sitting, crawling, and walking the infant may show developmental delay. Infants are innately sociable: they enjoy interacting with others, adults or children. A severely neglected infant will not have learnt the joy of reciprocal

---

Key features in infants

Physical	Failure to thrive
	Recurrent and persistent minor infections
	Frequent attendances at casualty departments or admissions to hospital
	Unexplained bruising
	Severe nappy rash
Development	General delay
Behaviour	Attachment disorders: anxious, avoidant
	Lack of social responsiveness

23

smiling and laughter and so may not try to elicit attention. Although the concept of infant depression is controversial, increasing evidence suggests that the infants of some depressed (and therefore comparatively neglectful) mothers do show characteristic social responses, such as withdrawal, "looking away" behaviour, and emotional flattening. Severely understimulated infants may use self stimulatory behaviours such as persistently banging their head or rocking.

Selective attachments to important adults in an infant's life begin to be established around 6 to 8 months of age. A neglected or abused infant may show an unusual pattern of attachment. Usually the experience of consistent and sensitive parenting leads a child to feel safe and secure with the primary caregiver, even in the presence of a stranger. In an unfamiliar setting such as a surgery or clinic the wish to explore will be counterbalanced by a wish to stay close to the parent. Infants who have been abused or neglected lack this sense of security. They do not have sufficient confidence to explore their surroundings and seem ill at ease, whining, and unhappy and cling to their caregiver, who responds with irritation. Alternatively, there may be little evidence for any attachment behaviour and the infant either roams around the room in a completely non-directed fashion (attributable perhaps to high anxiety) or creeps quietly into a corner and observes the proceedings warily (frozen watchfulness). Recent research has shown, however, that large differences in the availability of and nurture by a caregiver do not always correlate with variations in attachment.

Preschool children

The physical consequences of persistent abuse and neglect through the preschool period often include poor growth not only in height and weight but also in the circumference of the head. Dramatic increases in head size have been documented when abused children have been removed to a nurturing alternative environment. Associated indicators of abuse include recurrent minor unexplained injuries, especially bruising. It is important to be aware of the distribution of bruises that is likely to indicate squeezing, choking, and slapping.

The development of communication between children, even those who cannot talk, and their caregivers is a subtle process with its own set of shared expectations and rules of operation. Persistent neglect and abuse will prevent the establishment of a "mutual faith in a shared world." Retardation in the development of receptive and expressive language will result, possibly exacerbated by recurrent inadequately treated middle ear infections and partial deafness. When the emotional abuse has been severe a child may become virtually mute. Language development seems to be especially vulnerable to the effects of a severely depriving environment.

The main indicators of emotional abuse and neglect of preschool children are usually behavioural. As long as the child does not mix in a social setting no problems may be reported. In a

---

Key features in preschool children

Physical	Short stature
	Microcephaly
	Unkempt and dirty
Development	Language delayed
	Attention span limited
	Socioemotional immaturity
Behaviour	Overactive
	Aggressive and impulsive
	Indiscriminate friendliness
	Seeks physical contact from strangers

---

nursery school or day nursery, however, the child may show many and characteristic disorders. Attention span is commonly extremely limited: the child cannot settle to any task for more than a few seconds. This probably reflects a lack of attempts to engage the child's attention at home, but it may also indicate profound anxiety. Poor attention is often associated with excessive activity; such children may be described as hyperactive, although there is no evidence that most overactive preschool children have been abused. Aggressive disorders of conduct are an additional problem, and children who are observed persistently to hit or swear at their caregivers in the consulting room must be regarded as being at risk.

Peer relationships will inevitably be problematic as persistently abused children do not develop sufficient social maturity to play cooperatively. Therefore their relationships with other children may be characterised by a combination of aggression and withdrawal. Social relations will also be impaired by a lack of selective attachments; thus abused toddlers may show indiscriminately friendly behaviour that is qualitatively different from normal temperamental diversity and unlike behaviours reflective of broad social experience. Such children elicit intimate physical contact from complete strangers—they may end up on your lap within a few minutes of meeting—and seem to crave physical contact ("touch hunger"), even in the presence of their primary caregiver.

School children

In the child who has reached school age the effects of long term abuse and neglect occasionally lead to a characteristic syndrome of short stature coupled with certain behavioural and emotional problems. In many cases, however, there is no evidence of an effect on growth and the main indicators of abuse are to be found in poor social and emotional adjustment, behaviour problems, and learning difficulties.

School may be unable to compensate for the long term lack of cognitive stimulation at home because abused children have tremendous problems attending to learning tasks. The failure in concentration is often coupled with physical overactivity of such a degree that the child is regarded as disruptive and may be referred for assessment for special education.

Persistent denigration and rejection will inevitably cause a lowering of self esteem; children who feel they are worthless may carry a huge burden of guilt for their behaviour. They may seem depressed and persistently apologise for trivial or meaningless supposed misdemeanours. For example, an abused 5 year old seen recently at her first visit to a child guidance clinic apologised to the therapist for not having saved him a piece of her birthday cake; her birthday had been three months previously. Such a poor self image is not really compatible with forming and keeping friendships at school; the social skills needed to negotiate such relationships have never been learnt. Thus the emotionally abused child stands alone at playtime or is seen drifting around the periphery of small groups engaged in their own pursuits. Sometimes more able children develop a coping strategy whereby their main social interaction is with adults — that is, with teachers rather than pupils. They show a pseudomaturity that belies their lack of sense of self worth and their longing for affection and stability. When the abuse has been coupled with a style of interaction that is aggressive and threatening the child may show similar behaviour to pupils and teachers. Such behaviour may also be habitual because at home it is the only way of attracting attention.

In extreme cases of emotional abuse and neglect patterns of behaviour are so unusual or bizarre that they inevitably draw attention to the child. Self mutilation, from skin picking to deliberate self injury with knives or glass, is one. Repetitive rocking or other self stimulatory patterns of behaviour (including sexual ones) are others. Unusual patterns of defecation or urination are worrying in school children. Children who urinate or defecate in their clothes in class may be shunned as being smelly by their peers; perhaps that is how they view themselves — as disgusting and unpleasant individuals. Pools of urine or piles of faeces in the corridor or playground are signs that the culprit is urgently in need of assessment for possible abuse.

Key features in school children

Physical	Short stature Poor hygiene Unkempt appearance
Development	Learning difficulties Lack of self esteem Poor coping skills Socioemotional immaturity
Behaviour	Disordered or few relationships Self stimulating or self injurious behaviour, or both Unusual patterns of defecation or urination, or both

Investigation and management

Children who are being emotionally abused or neglected may not be in immediate physical or moral danger but their need for protection is not, for all that, diminished. It must be acknowledged, however, that there is limited scope in such cases for medical investigation without associated physical or sexual maltreatment. Doctors who suspect that a child is being abused should firstly seek the advice of a colleague who is experienced in such matters. If no local paediatrician or child psychiatrist is available an inquiry to a tertiary referral centre elsewhere in the county will often be met with a courteous and helpful response. Subsequently it will be necessary to share concerns with the statutory services responsible for child protection.

1 Department of Health and Social Security and the Welsh Office. *Working together. A guide to arrangements for inter-agency co-operation for the protection of children from abuse.* London: HMSO, 1988.

Further reading

Tronick EZ, Field T, eds. *Maternal deprivation and infant disturbance.* San Francisco: Jossey-Bass, 1986. (New directions for child development series No 34.)

Kagan J. Perspectives on infancy. In: Osofsky JD, ed. *Handbook of infant development.* 2nd ed. New York: Wiley, 1987:1150-98.

Marks HG, Borns P, Steg NL, Stine SB, Stroud HH, Vates TS. Catch-up brain growth—demonstration by CAT scan. *J Pediatr* 1978;**93**:254-7.

Skuse D. Extreme deprivation in early childhood. In: Bishop D, Mogford K, eds. *Language development in exceptional circumstances.* Edinburgh: Churchill Livingstone, 1988:29-46.

EMOTIONAL ABUSE AND DELAY IN GROWTH

David H Skuse

Better is a dinner of herbs where love is than
a stalled ox and hatred therewith

Proverbs xv, 17

Many exceptionally short children with no
detectable organic disorder to account for their
condition are that way because they have been—
and are usually continuing to be—abused within
their families. There may be no other physical
evidence of the abuse. The underlying aetiology
is probably always dysfunctional secretion of
growth hormone, but conventional
endocrinological studies may give misleading
results. The key to the diagnosis is a good history.
Failure to recognise this condition may imperil
not only the children's future physical
development but also their intelligence, their
social adjustment, and their emotional wellbeing.
Appreciable numbers of children newly referred
to specialist growth clinics have this seriously
underdiagnosed disorder, which is often known
as psychosocial dwarfism.

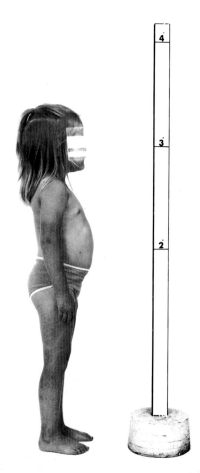

Girl aged 8 years 2½ months measuring 3' 4" (102 cm), a height age of 4 years

Defining features

The syndrome has no pathognomonic signs or
symptoms. It is the combination of current and
historical features that is characteristic. Some
aspects, such as behaviour around food, are fairly
easy to elicit at interview. Others, such as sexual
abuse, require skilled assessment by
appropriately trained staff. Not all features are
present in all children. The diagnosis is
confirmed by showing deficient secretion of
growth hormone and an abnormally low rate of
linear growth, both of which rapidly resolve
when the child is removed from the abusive
environment.

Anthropometry

A history of failure to thrive in infancy is
common. Height is usually far below the third
centile, although the child may be growing at a
low normal rate parallel to the centile line.
Occasionally the condition presents with a
variable and inconsistent growth trajectory.
Weight for height is appropriate and head
circumference and skinfold thickness are both
below average. Body proportions are immature
with comparatively short legs (figure). Siblings
and parents are often of average stature.

Feeding behaviour

A long history of disordered behaviour around
food is characteristic. Ask whether food is
"stolen" at home and preventive measures have
been taken—for example, locks on bedroom,
kitchen, and cupboard doors. Have there been
nocturnal forays in search of food to hoard in the
child's bedroom? Pica and the consumption of
discarded food found in street or wastebins can
lead to gastrointestinal disturbances (for which
specialist opinion may be sought). Are there
special arrangements to feed the child at home—
for example, separately from other family
members? Schoolteachers can often provide
valuable information. Ask parents what would
happen if they let the child eat as much as he or
she wanted in the expectation that you would be
told that the child would gorge until he or she
vomited.

Change of environment

Absolutely characteristic of the syndrome is
the observation that affected children show a
dramatic increase in linear growth once they have

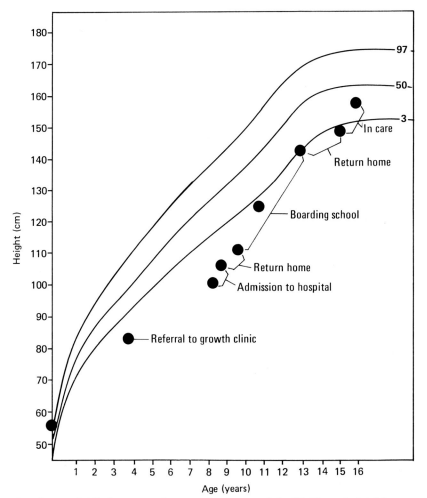

Growth curve of girl in figure on previous page related to events in her life. Her mother's height was 158 cm (25th centile) and her father's 178 cm (50th centile)

response with the local social services department is necessary. A case conference will be held and the services of other experts such as a child psychiatrist and paediatric endocrinologist may be deemed necessary. Legal proceedings are likely to be forthcoming to protect the child because it is unfortunately rare for the intrafamilial interactions to be amenable to treatment. If in court abuse is strenuously denied by the parents such cases may be notoriously difficult to prove. Evidence of accelerated linear growth in another environment, either in the past or since the intervention of the social services department, is then extremely valuable. Substantial growth away from home indicates that a child should not be returned, for obvious reasons.

Prevention

Although primary prevention may be impossible, increased vigilance by school doctors, general practitioners, and paediatricians should lead to an increased rate of diagnosis. So called deprivation dwarfism is no respecter of social or cultural boundaries. Although the consequences of acting on suspicions may be traumatic and far reaching, the consequence of turning a blind eye to the condition is often the stunting not only of growth but also of personality and intellect.

Urination and defecation

Unhappy, rejected and abused children may use urination and defecation as aggressive acts. All too often inappropriate professional advice has led to attempts at managing behaviour by star charts or bell and pad devices; such efforts are doomed to failure. Deliberate urination and the smearing of faeces at night over beds, toys, and furniture may indicate that the child's bedroom door has been locked. Defecation may occur in public places—for example, in school corridors or the playground; soiled pants may be hidden all over the house.

Developmental attainments

Because children with this condition are at best neglected and at worst rejected and unloved they have not experienced a close reciprocal and stimulating relationship with their parents. As a result their cognitive attainments show a deterioration over time as the impact of their environment assumes greater significance. Motor development will be less affected than skills based on language such as practical reasoning. Serial testing every six months or so, with a standardised instrument such as the Griffiths scales,[4] can yield valuable information. (Calculate scores as a percentage of mental age divided by chronological age to view trends.)

Social and emotional adjustment

Parents will often tell you that the child had a difficult temperament from the earliest days, would not settle into routines, was irritable, and

been removed from home. It is not unusual to find a sixfold to tenfold increase in the rate of growth within a few months.[1] Recent research has shown that on admission to hospital the pulse amplitude of nocturnal growth hormone secretion, which had been deficient, could become normal within three weeks.[2] The precise reasons for this are unclear. Mental development will also accelerate within months provided that an appropriate child-caregiver attachment is established and the child is encouraged to learn in a comparatively structured stimulating environment.[3] Odd behaviour patterns may, however, persist.

Should the child be returned home a diminution in growth rate will ensue. Unwary doctors may conclude that the potential for growth has been fulfilled, especially if the subsequent trajectory is parallel to the centile lines. Consider the growth curve above, which is the growth record of the girl shown on the previous page. Rapid increases in the growth in height during her admission to hospital and at boarding school were followed by stable linear growth. When she was 15 she ran away from home, and her height nearly reached the 25th centile.

Management

When a diagnosis of emotional abuse leading to a delay in growth is suspected a coordinated

Key features

- Age range toddlers to adolescents
- Proportionate stunting
- Feeding behaviour grossly disturbed
- Unusual patterns of urination and defecation
- Mental development delayed
- Poor social adjustment
- Unhappy, irritable, defiant
- Antisocial behaviour
- Parents' attitude critical or belittling, or both
- Associated abuse, especially sexual abuse
- Accelerated growth away from family
- Rapidly reversible growth hormone deficiency

disliked close physical contact. Relationships with parents and siblings are marked by sullen withdrawal or defiant hostility. At home and school an unhappy mood predominates. There are no close friends and self esteem is poor. Parental efforts at controlling undesirable behaviour are met with defiance and a seeming tolerance to most physical punishments. Some parents resort to bizarre techniques, often with sadistic overtones—for example, shutting fingers in drawers, beating the soles of the feet, making the child stand for prolonged periods with hands on head, and withdrawing food. Antisocial behaviours may be habitual, especially petty pilfering at school. In younger children apparently senseless destructive acts (smashing new toys) are indicative of inner turmoil and distress.

Parent-child relationship

The depth of the alienation in family relationships may not be gauged by a casual observer in the surgery or outpatient clinic. An abused child may nevertheless be brought for medical attention and investigations. You must not be deflected from a penetrating inquiry by the parents' seeming concern for the child's welfare. It is naive to imagine that emotional rejection and abuse are easily resolved by persuading the parents to give the child up to alternative caretakers. Quite apart from the possible role of that child as a focus for broader discontent within the family, parents may be exquisitely sensitive to the opinions of relatives and neighbours. They may fear the attentions of the police.

In addition to the emotional rejection and criticism—for example, telling an 8 year old child, "You've got custard for brains"—and the physical abuse to which I have alluded, doctors are becoming increasingly aware of the extent to which sexual abuse is a part of this syndrome. Sexual assaults may be incorporated into the regimen of punishments. Children may be subjected to a lifestyle that holds to few norms of socially acceptable behaviour. Both girls and boys are equally vulnerable.

1 Taitz LS, King JM. Growth patterns in child abuse. *Acta Paediatr Scand [Suppl]*1988;**343**:62-72.
2 Stanhope R, Adlard P, Hamill G, Jones J, Skuse D, Preece M. Physiological growth hormone (GH) secretion during the recovery from psychosocial dwarfism: a case report. *Clin Endocrinol (Oxf)* 1988;**28**:335-9.
3 Money J, Annecillo C, Kelley JF. Growth of intelligence: failure and catch-up associated respectively with abuse and rescue in the syndrome of abuse dwarfism. *Psychoneuroendocrinology* 1983;**8**:309-19.
4 Griffiths R. *The abilities of babies*. London: London University Press, 1954.

CHILD SEXUAL ABUSE—I

Frank Bamford, Raine Roberts

What is child sexual abuse?

Child sexual abuse is any use of children for the sexual gratification of adults.

Who abuses and who is abused?

The abuser is almost always a male known to the child: a relative (father, grandfather, uncle, or older brother); a member of the household (stepfather or mother's cohabitants); or a temporary carer—for example, teenage male babysitters. Note that abusing males may move after the discovery of abuse to another household of similar composition.

Child sexual abuse may occur in any part of society but is discovered more commonly in poor families.

Children of all ages and either sex may be sexually abused.

What happens?

Sexual abuse entails all types of sexual activity often with escalating intrusiveness.

Children may be exposed to indecent acts, pornographic photography, or external genital contact in the form of being fondled, masturbating an adult, or being used for intercrural intercourse. Finally, they may be penetrated orally, vaginally, or anally.

How often does sexual abuse occur?

Nobody knows how often sexual abuse occurs. It is certain that a lot of abuse is undiagnosed and equally certain that false diagnoses may be catastrophic.

Five main risk factors predispose to child sexual abuse.

● Previous incest or sexual deviance in the family

● New male member of the household with a record of sexual offences

● Loss of inhibition due to alcohol

● Loss of maternal libido or sexual rejection of father

● A paedophilic sexual orientation, especially in relation to sex rings and pornography.

Do children tell?

Sometimes children tell other people, but many are threatened to stop them telling. They may receive compensatory treats or presents.

Disclosure after a long period of abuse is common and may be followed by retraction. The statements of young children about sexual abuse should be taken seriously and, if possible, written down verbatim. Repeated questioning is potentially harmful and may evoke less truthful answers. Care is needed in understanding exactly what the child is saying—for example, "Daddy hurt my bum" may be interpreted in several ways, whereas "Daddy put his willie in my mouth" can hardly be anything other than abuse.

Does the non-abusing parent tell?

Sometimes the parent who is not sexually abusing the child will tell someone about the abuse, but collusion within families may occur, as in physical abuse. Beware of allegations made by parents in disputes about access or custody. Do not dismiss them but treat them with great caution.

What are the presenting symptoms?

Sexual abuse has three main types of presentation.

(1) Symptoms due to local trauma or infection—for example, perineal soreness, vaginal discharge, and anal pain or bleeding.

(2) Symptoms attributable to emotional effects—for example, loss of concentration, enuresis, encopresis, anorexia, and parasuicide. A change in behaviour is important.

(3) Sexualised conduct or inappropriate sexual knowledge of young children. Remember that such conduct or knowledge may be derived from observing others or from pornographic videos, but if a child describes pain or the quality of semen physical interference is probable.

Make careful notes at the time—they may be needed later as legal evidence.

What should be recorded?

Doctors dealing with child sexual abuse should keep a record of who asked them to see the child, who accompanied him or her, who raised the question of sexual abuse, who gave the history, and who was present at the examination.

The history should include details of the incident(s) causing suspicion; a full paediatric history, with particular emphasis on genitourinary or bowel symptoms; and details of previous abuse or sexual offences within the family or household.

Should the child be examined and where?

The child should be examined but not without the knowledge and agreement of a parent (or the order of a court). Mothers of preadolescent children should always be invited to be present, except in the most exceptional circumstances. Adolescent patients should be asked whether they wish a parent to be present.

It is usually counterproductive to examine a resistant child, and if his or her cooperation cannot be obtained the examination should be deferred unless there are urgent medical reasons to proceed.

The child should be examined as soon as optimal arrangements can be made. Few children require urgent examination.

Repetitive examination is usually abusive and should be avoided.

The examination should be conducted in absolute privacy and in an environment where the child can be comfortable—not behind screens in open wards or in police stations.

There should be adequate equipment for any necessary diagnostic tests. Recording and photographic facilities are an advantage but their value is outweighed if they cause distress to the child or mean that another examination has to be conducted.

Who should examine?

A person with skill in paediatric examination who is familiar with normal genital and anal appearances of children should conduct the examination. When physical abnormalities are expected from the history a forensic physician should be invited to examine or to be present during the examination so that it need not be repeated and a second opinion is available in doubtful cases.

Who should be present?

The only people present at the examination should be the child, his or her parent, and the examiner(s)—no one else—except, with the agreement of the parents, an occasional observer in training.

What about acute sexual abuse?

When abuse is thought to have been recent (within 72 hours) or there is serious genital injury forensic evidence must not be compromised. Examination should be deferred, if consistent with safety, until a forensic physician can be present. Nobody should remove clothing or attempt to clean or bath the child. Junior medical staff should not examine suspected victims unless the child urgently needs medical attention.

CHILD SEXUAL ABUSE—II

Frank Bamford, Raine Roberts

In child sexual abuse genital and anal examination should be in the context of a general clinical examination and include a search for other forms of abuse and an appraisal of growth, development, and health. The behaviour of the child in the presence of his or her parent should be noted.

Why should the genitalia be examined?

The genitalia should be examined in child sexual abuse for five main reasons.

- To detect traumatic or infective conditions that may require treatment
- To evaluate the nature of any abuse. Normal genital and anal appearances do not exclude the diagnosis, but in young children they make penetrative abuse unlikely
- To provide forensic evidence that may be helpful to the future protection of children
- To reassure the child, who sometimes feels that serious damage has been done
- To start the process of recovery.

How to examine the genitalia and anus

Cooperation during an examination is best achieved by telling children exactly what is happening and allowing them to feel in control by asking them to help. Let them take the swabs if they wish. The child may lie on her back for vulval inspection or on her side as for anal examination. With children up to 7 years old it is sometimes better for them to lie along the length of their mother's knee, facing forwards, with the mother gently flexing and abducting the hips. Adequate inspection requires a relaxed child.

Should fingers or a speculum be inserted?

Glaister's rods, if used gently in a cooperative child, may assist inspection of the edge of the hymen vaginalis but they are not absolutely necessary.

Some doctors insert a finger to assess the tone of the anal sphincter but unless there are clear indications of abuse it should be avoided. Views differ as to its importance.

In a small number of cases in which vaginal examination or repair is necessary the child should be given a general anaesthetic. General anaesthesia should also be considered if there is vaginal bleeding after suspected abuse.

Can sexual abuse be proved by clinical examination?

Semen or blood of a group different from that of the child would if present within the vagina or rectum, or on the perineum in a prepubertal child, be conclusive evidence of interference, but such cases are uncommon in forensic practice and wholly exceptional in paediatric practice. Lubricants or hairs are of similar importance. Genital infection with *Neisseria gonorrhoeae* is indicative of contact with an infected person in 98% of cases, but all other findings can be produced by circumstances or conditions other than sexual abuse. It follows that, with the exceptions mentioned, the concept of a single, conclusive, diagnostic sign is invalid.

How patent is a child's vagina?

The likelihood or otherwise of penetration may be inferred from the size of the hymenal orifice.

Right: Examine small children on their mother's knee

Far right: Glaister's rods: graduated glass globes of different sizes

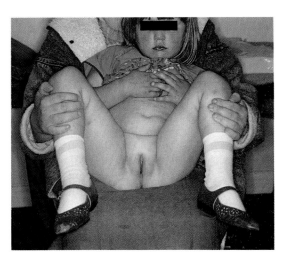

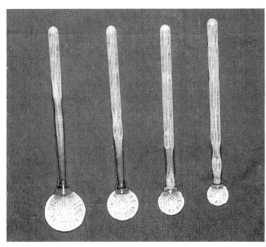

Right: Swabs for detection of sexually transmitted disease may be important; when possible let the child keep control and take swabs

Far right: Tear of hymen, left lateral, would have been missed without use of Glaister's rod

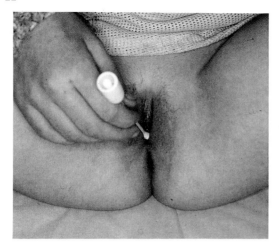

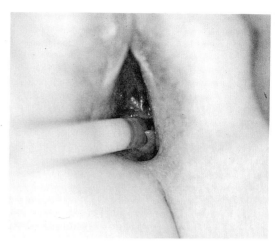

Individual hymens vary substantially from the imperforate to the congenitally absent, and the hymen may occasionally be cribriform. In most prepubescent children it is a membrane with a circular or crescentic opening and a smooth, regular margin that may be either thin or rounded.

The diameter is difficult to measure accurately but in most young children the unstretched hymenal orifice is no more than 0·5-0·6 cm. The diameter increases as puberty is approached. As the diameter of an adult index finger is about 1·5 cm and that of an erect penis two or three times greater an intact unstretched hymen precludes the possibility of penetration.

It is important to spend some time carefully observing the hymen before coming to any conclusion about it. A hymen appearing small and undamaged will sometimes open up as the child relaxes and tears and bumps may be seen.

What causes irregularity or tearing of the hymen?

The hymen may be damaged in four main ways.

- By sexual abuse
- By genital disease. A careful history is important
- By self injury. This is unusual because it is painful, but damage to the hymen may occur by the insertion of foreign bodies
- By accidental injury. This is also unusual because after infancy the introitus is protected by the labia.

Signs of intercrural intercourse

There are usually no signs of intercrural intercourse. It may cause patchy redness of the labia and perineum, but this is common in other conditions—for example, enuresis and poor hygiene. The rounded labial contour may be flattened, but it is not a reliable sign as flattening can be due to tight clothing. There may be a split of the posterior fourchette and a subsequent scar. Finally, the pressure of a penis against the hymen may stretch it and the child may think that there has been penetration.

Petechial brusing on palate. Always look in mouth for signs of oral sex

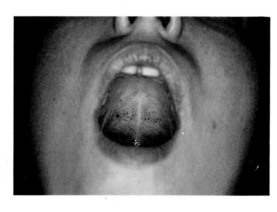

Below: Be careful not to mistake vestibule for hymen. On left vestibule is seen while on right closer picture of same child shows red crescent of hymen

Signs of buggery

The signs of buggery are likely to be most prominent in young children. There may be no abnormal signs but look for evidence of external trauma, skin changes, and anal dilatation.

External trauma in anal abuse

Perineal bruising or bleeding without a reasonable explanation raises substantial suspicions of abuse. They need to be distinguished from haemangiomas.

Fissures due to overstretching of the sphincter may be multiple and radiate. Their extent is probably in proportion to the disparity in size between the assailant and the child and the degree of force used, and they may leave scars and sometimes anal skin tags. Be careful to distinguish fissures from prominent folds in the anal canal.

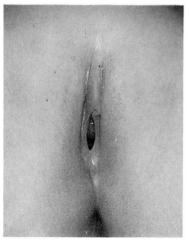

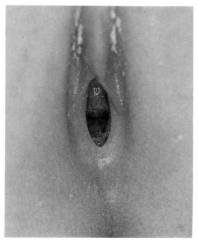

Perianal skin changes

Swelling of the skin around the anal verge may be seen occasionally after recent abuse and thickening after repeated abuse. The skin of the anal verge may become rounded and smooth. Distinguish from lichen sclerosus et atrophicus, perianal moniliasis, and scratching by children infected with threadworms. Skin changes by themselves are not sufficient to lead to investigation of abuse.

Veins in the skin may become dilated giving a bruised appearance. Back pressure from the inferior rectal veins is implied and may be seen in abuse, but great caution is needed in interpretation, especially if there is any possibility of a bowel disorder.

Warts around the anus (or vaginal introitus) may be transmitted by genital contact. They are strongly suggestive of sexual abuse, especially if wart virus of a genitally transmitted type is

VARIATIONS IN HYMEN

Right: Two holes in hymen

Far right top: Septate hymen. Bands are usually vertical. Hymenal tags (not shown) may be incomplete bands and be mistaken for tears

Far right below: Bump on hymen. Hymen has probably been torn posteriorly leaving bumps and slight thickening

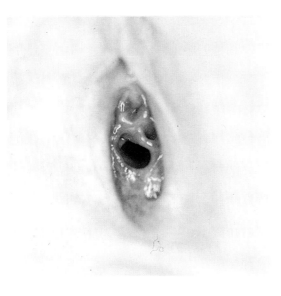
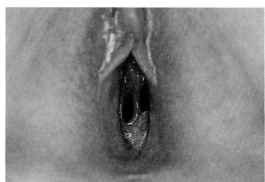
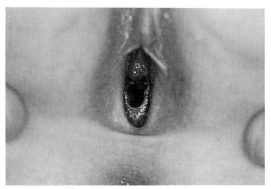

CLASSIC INJURY OF ATTEMPTED PENILE PENETRATION

Right: Haematoma of hymen and split of posterior fourchette

Far right top: Recently torn hymen in teenage girl. Hymen usually tears in posterior half

Far right below: Flattening of labia inferiorly. This may be caused by abuse from penis being pushed repeatedly against labia but may also be normal or caused by wearing nappies

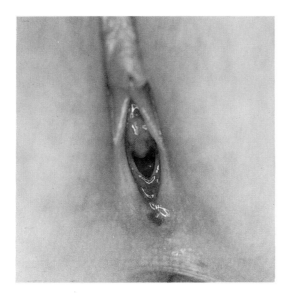
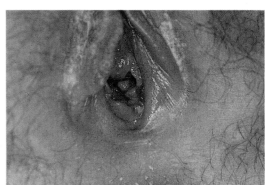
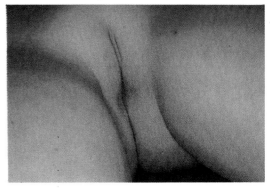

Inflamed, thickened hymen, in this case caused by rubbing

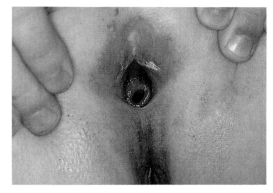

Redness caused by rubbing

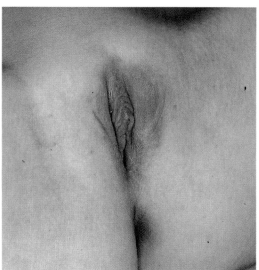

the anus, but it is impossible to be sure whether the object has passed upwards or come downwards. A history of bowel problems or of medical investigation or treatment is therefore important. "Reflex" anal dilatation is not a true reflex. It amounts to relaxation of the anal sphincter about 10 seconds after the anus has been inspected so that an initially closed anus opens during the course of examination (alternatively an anus open at first closes during the examination and then opens again).

Anal closure and continence is dependent upon the internal anal sphincter. If it is incompetent because of stretching or injury there is likely to be soiling. The internal anal sphincter may be relaxed physiologically by faeces in the lower rectum. In examining children in whom abuse is suspected it is important to ensure that they are relaxed, that the rectum is empty, and that there is no other source of pressure on it. When the internal sphincter is incompetent the external sphincter may be able to maintain closure for a short time but cannot sustain it, hence the changes seen during examination. "Reflex" anal dilatation may be a pointer to sexual abuse but is not reliable as a sole diagnostic sign and its significance is currently unproved.

identified. Genital warts are usually smaller than common warts and appear as multiple papules along the inner surface of the labia or circumferentially around the anus. They occur particularly where skin is moist. Parents or children who have common warts on their hands may infect skin in the region of the genitalia or anus during toileting.

Anal dilatation

Given that the bowel is normal and that the child does not suffer from any neurological disorder, abnormal patency is indicative of something hard and large having passed through

Should tests be done for sexually transmitted disease?

Sexually transmitted disease should always be tested for in children molested by strangers. In intrafamilial cases obtain swabs unless it is clearly going to cause distress. Sometimes it is helpful to get suspected abusing parents to attend a genitourinary medicine clinic.

Taking a low vaginal swab at the initial examination is usually appropriate, but it may need to be repeated within 10 days of contact. Prepubertal children with gonorrhoea have acute vaginitis and cervical or high vaginal swabs are not needed. Repetitive swabbing is usually unnecessary but serological tests for syphilis and chlamydia should be done six weeks or more after the last contact. Tests for antibodies to HIV may be required later in specific cases, as may pregnancy tests in postpubertal girls.

ANAL DILATATION

Right: Place hands gently on buttocks and wait

Far right: Both sphincters open. Do not pull with fingers as false positive results will occur. Ensure rectum is empty. (Note that faeces can be seen in this girl's rectum)

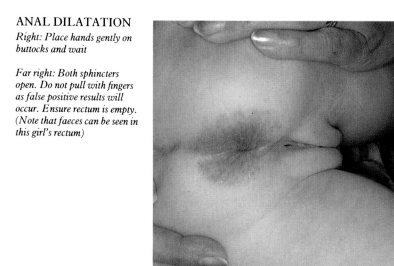

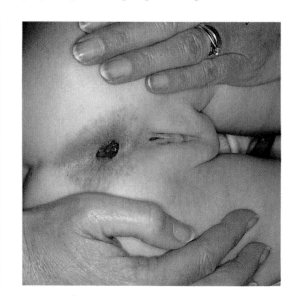

Buggery: Top pictures show swelling, bruising, and fissures of anal margin caused by recent buggery

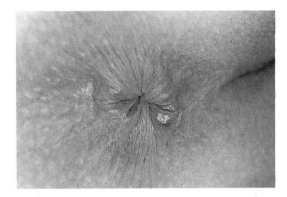 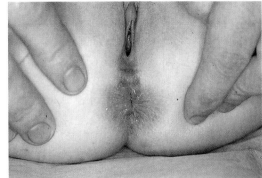

Right: Anal dilatation, bruising and fissure

Far right: Appearance of healed anus 10 days later

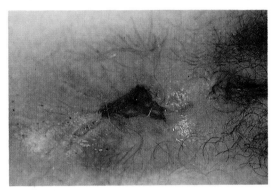 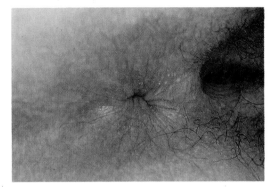

Medical management

The medical management of child sexual abuse is part of an interdisciplinary process. Communication with other agencies is essential.

Possible sexual abuse

(1) If child sexual abuse is only a possibility— for example, the child has made a vague statement, there are behavioural changes, vulval or anal soreness, or family risk factors—take a careful history from the carer and write down anything said by the child but do not engage in an intrusive interview.

(2) If the history points to a probability of abuse refer the child to an experienced person.

(3) If the history is not clearly indicative of abuse examine the whole child, including the genitalia, and take swabs if appropriate.

(4) Discuss the case with colleagues in the practice, including health visitors and possibly school nurses. Hospital doctors should discuss the case with the family's general practitioner. Some regions have experienced staff who are willing to advise. Ascertain whether the family are known by or have caused concern to the social services.

(5) Tell the carer of your findings and opinion.

(6) Arrange follow up visits and ensure that appointments are kept.

Probable sexual abuse

(1) If child sexual abuse is probable because of a clear statement from the child or unexplained recent vaginal or anal injury inform the police and social services department promptly, with the knowledge and, if possible, the agreement of the carer.

(2) Do not examine the child—arrange for a full, single paediatric and forensic examination at which suitable samples and photographs can be obtained.

(3) Check that the medical welfare of the child

*Genital and anal findings which **may** indicate abuse*

Redness or swelling of clitoris

Stretching or tearing of hymen

Bumps or irregularities of hymen

Bands or synechiae

Adhesions of labia minora

Splits or scarring of posterior fourchette

Perianal or perivulval warts

Perineal or perianal bruising or petechiae

Fissures and scars

Lax sphincter Dilatation

Skin changes due to rubbing

Child sexual abuse—II

Treatment of cases of child sexual abuse by primary care doctors (based on chart from "Physician")

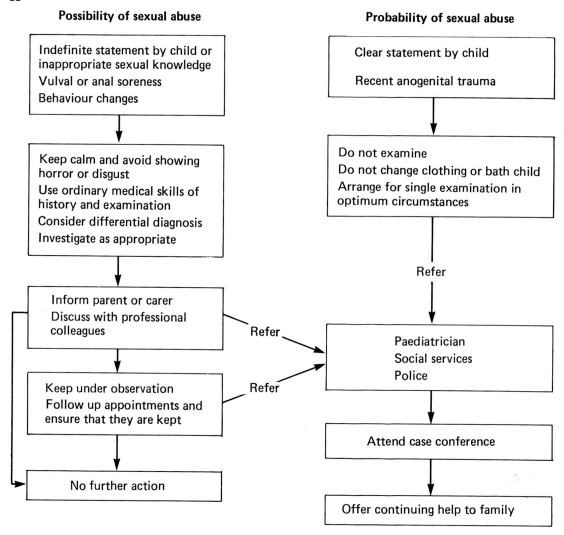

Possibility of sexual abuse

> Indefinite statement by child or inappropriate sexual knowledge
> Vulval or anal soreness
> Behaviour changes

↓

> Keep calm and avoid showing horror or disgust
> Use ordinary medical skills of history and examination
> Consider differential diagnosis
> Investigate as appropriate

↓

> Inform parent or carer
> Discuss with professional colleagues

↓

> Keep under observation
> Follow up appointments and ensure that they are kept

↓

> No further action

Probability of sexual abuse

> Clear statement by child
> Recent anogenital trauma

↓

> Do not examine
> Do not change clothing or bath child
> Arrange for single examination in optimum circumstances

Refer ↓

> Paediatrician
> Social services
> Police

↓

> Attend case conference

↓

> Offer continuing help to family

Refer (from "Inform parent or carer" box to "Paediatrician/Social services/Police" box)
Refer (from "Keep under observation" box to "Paediatrician/Social services/Police" box)

---

has been safeguarded—that is, infections treated and, if appropriate, pregnancy tests and postcoital contraception provided.

(4) Facilitate interviews of the child by a psychiatrist, psychologist, police officer, or social worker agreed by all the parties concerned. Avoid further abuse of the child by preventing different people going over the same material repetitively.

(5) Ascertain whether there are other children at risk and arrange to examine them.

(6) Participate in a multidisciplinary case conference.

(7) Ensure long term follow up with child psychiatrists as appropriate.

Allegations by an adult against another

When an adult accuses another adult of child sexual abuse refer the case to an experienced person because such cases often lead to litigation.

Violent sexual assault outside the family

Refer all cases in which children are violently assaulted outside the family to the police.

Do not touch or examine the child, except in an emergency.

Ensure the medical welfare of the child as in other cases but after forensic examinations are complete.

Almost all victims require skilled psychiatric help.

Confidentiality

The overriding duty is to the child. It is usually possible to obtain the consent of one parent to examination and disclosure—in any event you are obliged to make sure that the parent(s) understand that information will be shared.

Further reading

Department of Health and Social Security. *Diagnosis of child sexual abuse: guidance for doctors.* London: HMSO, 1988.
Ciba Foundation. Porter R, ed. *Child sexual abuse within the family.* London: Tavistock, 1987.

MUNCHAUSEN SYNDROME BY PROXY

Roy Meadow

RAISING THE COLLEGE OF PHYSICIANS

Baron von Munchausen, born in 1720, was a German mercenary and a gifted raconteur. Richard Asher in 1951 dedicated the Munchausen syndrome to the memory of the baron because the patients had his characteristic of travelling widely and telling false stories.

The picture shows Baron von Munchausen raising the College of Physicians of London into the air for three months, during which the health of its patients was never better

Munchausen syndrome by proxy was used first in 1977 to describe children whose mothers invented stories of illness about their child and substantiated the stories by fabricating false physical signs.

The Munchausen syndrome is applied to adults who invent false stories of illness about themselves, thereby incurring needless investigations and treatments. For children affected by the Munchausen syndrome by proxy the proxy is the mother, who provides the false information. Child abuse results partly from the direct actions of the mother — for example, giving drugs to make the child unconscious — and partly from those of doctors, who arrange invasive investigations or needless treatments for a child at the mother's instigation.

In the past 10 years the boundaries of this type of abuse have been found to be wide and to overlap with other forms of abuse; it manifests in four main ways: perceived illness, doctor shopping, enforced invalidism, and fabricated illness.

Perceived illness

Anxious parents may worry needlessly that their healthy child is ill. A mother who is inexperienced, under stress, lonely, or herself ill is all the more likely to perceive symptoms in her child that others do not observe. The child is taken to doctors, perhaps on many occasions, if she cannot be reassured. Often the child will have unpleasant investigations and treatments because of the mother's insistence. Most doctors, however, would not classify this process as child abuse unless the mother's persistence and refusal to accept normal results was excessive and the quality of the child's life was being seriously impaired.

Doctor shopping

Some parents shop around or seek help from a succession of different doctors. They may do this within the NHS or privately by paying for consultations. They persist in claiming that their healthy child is ill, and as each doctor in turn refuses further investigation they consult yet another doctor. The result for the child is a series of repetitive investigations and unpleasant venepunctures and a body that has been thoroughly irradiated and biopsied. When a parent's conviction about illness reaches these delusional proportions it results in child abuse.

Enforced invalidism

Some parents who have an ill or disabled child seek to keep the child ill, increase the degree of disability, or ensure that the child is regarded as incapacitated (when he or she is not). Thus the parents of a child with normal intelligence who has difficulty with spelling may insist that their child is mentally disabled and persuade the education authorities to accept the child into a special school. Alternatively, parents of children with a mild hemiplegia may insist that they spend their time in a wheelchair and bring them up to believe that they cannot walk, when they can.

The link with school refusal and school phobia is obvious. In many cases the child is being brought up to believe that he or she is ill and to miss school. Normally when a child is absent from school for an extended time the education authorities have the power to force the parents to return the child to education, but the difficulty for the education authorities is that these children have a genuine medical problem and the parents can persuade the education authorities that the disability from the child's illness is greater than it is; teaching or a special school may then be arranged.

Dealing with perceived illness, doctor shopping, and enforced invalidism

When dealing with perceived illness, doctor shopping, or enforced invalidism the doctor should bear in mind that these types of behaviour are an extension of the usual way that many parents behave when their child is ill. As with all forms of child abuse, it is the degree of abuse that matters. For a worried parent to seek a second or third specialist opinion is reasonable: to seek a 22nd opinion is not. As doctors, we have to listen carefully to parents' worries and to believe them when they say that their child is ill. We have to work within the framework of parents' expectations and experience of health to help them to come to understand and accept their child's behaviour and health. No one will blame a mother who keeps her child away from school an extra day or two because her child has a chronic illness or disability. Most of us accept the strategies that parents adopt to deal with chronic illness within their family, even when we do not agree with them: if the mother believes that a special diet will lessen the number of seizures of her epileptic child then it is unreasonable to interfere unless the diet is definitely nutritionally unsound or very inconvenient. If the child is

Munchausen syndrome by proxy

being forced to sleep on the back of an upturned cupboard enclosed in aluminium foil to avoid suspected allergens, however, the strategy amounts to child abuse and interference is necessary.

With such families early cooperation with health visitors and also social services may be helpful. For hospital doctors close consultation with the general practitioner is needed because only the general practitioner may be aware of the many other specialists previously consulted. If the parents cannot be dissuaded by careful and sympathetic help from their perceptions and actions that are harming their child then child abuse procedures should be invoked.

Fabricated illness

Fabricated or factitious illness results from parents who lie to the doctor about their child's health and from those who fabricate physical signs or alter health records. Some parents do all these things, but it can be equally serious for the child if the parent merely relates persistently and realistically a convincing history of illness—for example, many epileptic seizures each week—for the story alone will cause the doctor to embark on detailed investigations and prescribe anticonvulsant treatment. Parents invent the false illness while the child is young—usually starting within the first two years. They may continue and intensify the story of illness as the years pass. If the deception is not uncovered before the child is of school age some children will

participate in the deception. The mother teaches the child to trick the doctors and to lie. Some children subsequently have become independent illness addicts and have grown up to have the Munchausen syndrome.

There are five main consequences for children who are falsely labelled as ill.

(1) They will receive needless and harmful investigations and treatments.

(2) A genuine disease may be induced by the mother's actions—for example, renal failure as a result of regular injections of immunisation agents given to cause fever.

(3) They may die suddenly as a result of the mother misjudging the degree of insult. Mothers who, for example, partially suffocate their children to cause unconsciousness may smother the child for too long thereby causing brain damage or death.

(4) They may develop chronic invalidism. The child accepts the illness story and believes himself to be disabled and unable to attend school, to work, or even to walk.

(5) They may develop Munchausen syndrome as an adult—the children have learnt and then taken over the lying behaviour of their mother.

The stories of false illness usually concern the common chronic disorders of childhood: recurrent seizures, diarrhoea and vomiting, rashes, allergy, and fevers. Often they include more dramatic items such as recurrent bleeding.

In many instances the mother confirms the false history with false signs. The table lists some false signs together with the usual ways in which they are caused.

The consequences may be serious: some children have been in hospital for more than 18 months, during which their mothers have continued to lie and to fabricate signs; others have been absent from school for more than two years or have had lengthy periods of parenteral feeding, intravenous drug treatments, and large amounts of inappropriate drugs, including corticosteroids and cytotoxic agents.

In nearly all cases the mother is the deceiver: the father does not know what is going on. The mother tends to be the dominant person in the marriage and to be more intelligent and capable than her husband. The husband tends to be in the background, getting on with his own life and unsupportive of his wife's needs. The mothers often have had a difficult childhood themselves, and many have worked as nurses. About a fifth of the mothers are personal illness addicts and are notorious for presenting with unexplained illnesses.

The mothers usually keep to one general practitioner and when referred to hospital to one specialist. The referrals to other specialists come from the general practitioner or the hospital specialist. For the more complicated cases the children are transferred from centre of excellence to centre of excellence, where they undergo repetitive examination. The mother thrives on this, accompanying the child to the different hospitals, and is an avid consumer of good facilities for resident mothers.

Many of the mothers have had formal

Fabricated illnesses

False sign	Cause
Seizures, apnoea, and drowsiness	Poisons, suffocation, pressure on neck
Bleeding (haematuria, haematemesis, etc)	Blood from mother (particularly vaginal tampon), raw meat, or from child added to sample from child or smeared around child's nose, vulva, etc Colouring agents added to sample or smeared on to child Warfarin administration
Fever	Warming thermometer Altering temperature chart Injections of contaminated material into child's vein Repetitive injections of antigenic material
Diarrhoea	Laxatives
Vomiting	Mechanically induced Salt or emetic poisoning
Hypertension	Altering blood pressure chart or instructions concerning size of cuff for blood pressure estimation
Rashes	Scratching the skin to cause blisters Caustics and dyes
Renal stone	Addition of stone to child's urine to which blood has previously been added
Faeculent vomits	Making child vomit and stirring in faeces
Failure to thrive and thinness	Withholding food If in hospital and child is parenterally fed interfering with treatment and sucking back stomach contents through nasogastric tube

Action on suspicion of factitious illness

- Check history in detail—obtain verification of events alleged to have occurred in presence of third parties
- Seek temporal association between events and mother's presence
- Check personal, social, and family history—often the mother will have lied about them
- Contact other family members and doctors or health workers concerned
- Seek a motive—What is the mother gaining from making her child ill?

In hospital

- Secure and verify charts and records
- Retain and analyse samples—for example, blood and urine samples for toxicology
- Increase surveillance
- Participate with social services
- Exclude mother (aim for voluntary exclusion, though legal enforcement may be required)

Motive

The motives vary. For most mothers there is personal gain in terms of status, contacts with helpful doctors, nurses, and social workers, financial benefits, contact with other mothers and a different society in hospital, escape from an unhappy marriage, or the capture of an absent husband to share a problem. After talking with many of these mothers my main impression is of their unusual selfishness: they are able to do horrific things to children because of their own unhappiness and to satisfy their own needs. In a minority, particularly those who indulge in suffocation or poisoning, there commonly is envy of, and violence and hatred towards, the abused child.

Action and reaction

At one end of its range fabricated illness is as serious as any other type of abuse and calls for prompt liaison with social services, and sometimes the police, to protect the child. It is, however, important not to overreact just because a mother is lying or fabricating signs. Sometimes a mother may add blood to her child's urine or alter a temperature chart to dissuade the doctors from discharging her child from hospital before she is sufficiently reassured and ready to cope. Such minor events are common and should be sorted out sympathetically and promptly in a way that dissuades the mother from giving false histories or fabricating signs again.

The doctor discovering deception has to stand back for a moment and work out exactly how much the child is being harmed by the mother's direct and indirect actions and then discuss those factors with social services.

psychiatric assessment and most are considered not to have a mental illness, though they have a personality disorder.

Warning signs

In a minority of families other siblings are similarly affected and in a few families there has been non-accidental injury or unexplained death of other children.

Some of the warning signs that should alert a doctor to fabricated illness are listed below.

(1) The illness is unexplained, prolonged, or extremely rare.

(2) The symptoms and signs have a temporal association with the mother's presence. They may also be incongruous—for example, blood stained vomit from a child who is pink and laughing and has a full volume pulse.

(3) The mother is a hospital addict and more anxious to impress the doctor than she is worried about her child's illness.

(4) The treatment prescribed is ineffective and not tolerated.

(5) In the family there are multiple illnesses and similar symptoms in other members of the family.

Further reading

Meadow R. Munchausen syndrome by proxy. *Arch Dis Child* 1982; 57: 92-8.
Meadow R. Fictitious epilepsy. *Lancet* 1984;ii:25-8.
Meadow R. Management of Munchausen syndrome by proxy. *Arch Dis Child* 1985;**60**:385-93.
Mitchels B. Munchausen syndrome by proxy—protection or correction. *New Law Journal* 1983;**133**:165-8.
Rosenberg DA. Web of deceit: a literature review of Munchausen syndrome by proxy. *Child Abuse Negl* 1987;**11**:547-63.
Waller DA. Obstacles to the treatment of Munchausen by proxy syndrome. *Journal of the American Academy of Child Psychiatry* 1983;**22**:80-5.

ROLE OF THE CHILD PSYCHIATRY TEAM

A R Nicol

The child psychiatry team may consist of various professionals in different districts but commonly includes a clinical psychologist, social worker, community nurse, occupational therapist, specialist teacher, and non-medical psychotherapist as well as a consultant child psychiatrist.

Why should child psychiatrists be concerned with child abuse?

As the long term damage resulting from child abuse is overwhelmingly on the child's emotional development the relevance of child psychiatry and psychology is obvious.

Below is a simplified table of some of the adverse emotional and behavioural effects associated with child abuse together with their potential outcomes in later childhood and adult life. It should be emphasised that these outcomes are not inevitable: many can probably be modified by favourable later experience or by specific treatment.

It should be the task of the team managing child abuse, particularly the child psychiatrist, to try to prevent these damaging long term consequences.

How and when should child psychiatrists become active in child abuse?

There are several points in the management of child abuse at which child psychiatry should be considered. A child psychiatrist is particularly likely to be helpful when he or she has extensive experience of this particularly difficult and sometimes unpleasant type of work.

Assessment

The broad range of experience that is built into the training of a child psychiatrist is relevant to the assessment of a family when child abuse is suspected or has occurred. A child psychiatrist may be particularly helpful when both the following circumstances are true. Firstly, the child or other children in the family show signs of emotional problems, behavioural difficulties, or developmental delays; one or both parents seem to show evidence of personality disorder (very common) or of mental illness (less common, about 10% of cases); or there are questions about the quality of family relationships. Secondly, the professionals concerned with the case are puzzled about aspects of the diagnosis or they require guidance on how to proceed in the face of uncertainty.

Court work

The training of psychiatrists in assessing psychological problems and describing the intangibles of emotional life should equip them to provide a formulation of a problem of child abuse that will be well adapted to presenting evidence in court as either a material or an expert witness.

General management

Child psychiatrists are familiar with the principles of child care. These principles include the fact that decisions about child care should be made quickly and plan for the long term and that the psychological parent need not be the same person as the biological parent.

These principles should be imprinted on the consciousness of all those who try to help children in distress. Child psychiatrists, however, will have long and many faceted experience of their implications in practice. They may be able to complement or support social workers and other staff, partly through their long experience in practice but also because of their independence from the local authority hierarchy. Child psychiatrists should play a part in case conferences and planning the management of any cases in which he or she has become involved. This will include taking part in decisions about whether the child should return to the family or be brought up in an alternative family and also about specific management and treatment.

Specific management

Several specific treatments are relevant to problems that may arise in child abuse.

Childhood experience	Possible outcome
Repeated separations	Problems in making and sustaining intimate personal relationships Reactive depression
Neglect and understimulation	Developmental delays
Excessive punitiveness	Passive, "frozen" behaviour Disorganised aggressiveness
Inadequate discipline and family disorganisation	Delinquency, immaturity, poor habit training—for example, encopresis
Family discord and distorted family relationships	Manipulativeness, conduct disorder
Sexual exploitation	Sexual dysfunction, low self esteem

- Specific treatment may be needed for a parent with a mental illness. In this case a child psychiatrist may call on the help of a colleague who is an adult psychiatrist, but the child psychiatrist may have a deeper appreciation of the impact on the family of mental illness in parents and a greater experience of child abuse.
- Specific focused psychological intervention using behaviour modification principles may be useful when the abuse is associated with an extremely poor quality of parenting in the family. This may be undertaken by the social worker, clinical psychologist, or child psychiatrist but a support team is helpful in planning treatment and providing continuity.
- Anger management programmes are a way of helping people who have difficulty controlling their aggressive impulses. They can be useful when the abuser is, for example, an impulsive young man who is horrified at what he has done and thus well motivated to change. This is not an uncommon finding.
- Sexual abuse gives rise to some of the greatest psychological problems. Well run groups for older children or adolescent victims or play therapy for younger children may be a great help; counselling for other family members may also be helpful, and self help groups have been described but little used in this country.
- Family approaches can be useful in both physical and sexual abuse but need to be used with caution and when the aim of the treatment is clear. Abusive families are families full of fear and mistrust. The indiscriminate use of conjoint family approaches—that is, those in which the whole family is seen together—is naive and silly. There is no place for it.

These specific interventions should be subordinate to the overall treatment and management programme for the child and family. The process and results of treatment need to be carefully documented because apart from the specific benefits of the treatment they may contribute invaluable information about the capacity and motivation of the family for change and hence contribute to the major multidisciplinary decisions that need to be made about the family at case conferences.

Summary

In summary, a child psychiatrist can make an important contribution to the management of child abuse. At least one child psychiatrist in each district should take an interest in this work and should be given the time to do so. As for other professionals, child abuse is an aspect of the work of child psychiatrists that is particularly harrowing and time consuming.

Further reading

Nicol AR. The treatment of child abuse in the home environment. In: Browne K, Davies C, Stratton P, eds. *Early prediction and prevention of child abuse*. Chichester: Wiley, 1988.
Kelly JA. *Treating child abusive families—intervention based on skills training principles*. New York: Plenum, 1983.
Giarreto H. A comprehensive child sexual abuse treatment programme. In: Mrazek PB, Kempe CH, eds. *Sexually abused children and their families*. Oxford: Pergamon, 1981.

CASE CONFERENCES

Jill McMurray

In 1980 the Department of Health and Social Security issued a circular that gave advice to social services and other agencies on setting up a more systematic approach to the management of child abuse. It included new extended criteria for registering children who had been or were suspected of being abused and also extended the upper age range to 17 years. It recommended that issues be discussed by an interagency "case conference" (not to be confused with the informal meetings known as case discussions). The circular emphasised particularly the responsibility of all agencies concerned with children to consider the interests of children as paramount and gave special directions to agencies in which child protection was a major part of their work.

There are three agencies with statutory responsibility for child protection: the local authority (through the social service departments), the National Society for the Prevention of Cruelty to Children, and the police.

If information is received by any of these agencies that a child has been or is likely to be ill treated it has a duty and responsibility to investigate and if necessary take steps to protect the child.

A case conference is called as soon as possible when abuse has been confirmed or is suspected (in Scotland no further major changes concerning the child may be made, including reviewing the child, without a subsequent case conference being called).

Case conferences

Case conferences are valuable in bringing people together with relevant information, and in including them in planning and decision making. A case conference may be requested by any professional, but the decision to hold one is usually taken by the chairman (check who chairs and convenes in areas you cover). He or she has responsibility for invitations to case conferences

Doctors cannot be compelled to attend case conferences.
Information exchanged at a case conference has no guarantee of confidentiality.
A breach of confidence to the child and his parents may be justified if it is believed to be in the child's best interests.
CATHERINE JAMES, *Journal of the Medical Defence Union*, 1988

but tell him or her if you are aware of people with contributions to make—for example, radiologists, ward sisters, or nurses. The chairman will need a medical report from doctor(s) who examined the child(ren).

Check if a child or children in the family have previously attended a hospital, including an accident and emergency department. Advise the chairman that copies of your report should not be circulated without your permission.

Check if parents are allowed to attend. Most are not.

The Scottish circular emphasises how important it is that consultants recognise the interests of children as paramount and how vital it is for general practitioners, health visitors, consultants, etc, to attend case conferences. It also advises that case conferences should be held "before a child leaves hospital for home or any place of safety." The recommendation of compulsory measures requires the conference to refer the case to the reporter for consideration about whether it should go before a children's hearing.

Emergency procedures

If you think that a child will probably be reinjured or removed from hospital or the area by his or her parents you can request any of the three agencies with statutory responsibilities to seek a place of safety order, which currently may last up to a maximum of 28 days but is often shorter. (A report will be needed from a doctor.) The National Society for the Prevention of Cruelty to Children or social services will usually interview the parents and discuss the case with you before obtaining the order.

The request is taken to a magistrate, who will decide if an order should be granted. A copy of the order should be kept in the ward if the child is in hospital. The parents will also receive a copy.

A decision not to apply for care proceedings by the agency or case conference will allow a place of safety order to lapse. To apply for care

---

Child protection register

One of the commonest outcomes of a case conference is for the child to be placed on the child protection register (formerly called the "at risk register"). Sometimes other children within the household will also be placed on the register at the same time. The register is kept by the social services department and any doctor may telephone the local social services department at any time of the day or night to check whether a particular child is on it. This is a helpful diagnostic procedure when a doctor encounters a child for the first time in whom he suspects possible abuse. Even if the family move to another locality the child will be transferred automatically to the child protection register in the new locality.

Tasks of case conferences

- To examine information and evidence of abuse and being at risk (from medical and social work reports)
- To consider whether legal action is needed immediately to protect the child
- To consider the position of other children in the family
- To consider families' ability to protect children and to cooperate with the help offered
- To assess type of help available to the family—for example, day nursery, family aide, counselling, voluntary supervision
- To make provisional plans for working with the family
- To decide on registration of child(ren) and category
- To appoint a focal agency
- To decide who will inform the parents of case conference decisions
- To arrange for review and follow up (including medical when necessary)

proceedings, however, the juvenile court will fix a date for the hearing. Courts vary in whether they require you to attend. The court can (*a*) make a care order that applies until the child is 18 years of age unless it is revoked earlier (children may be returned home while remaining under the jurisdiction of a care order), (*b*) make a supervision order (child usually returns home), or (*c*) dismiss the case.

Other children in the family may be committed to care if the case is proved for the first child.

Children appearing in care proceedings often have a guardian ad litem appointed and a solicitor to look after their interests and not those of the parents, the social services department, or the National Society for the Prevention of Cruelty to Children. The police no longer takes children to court under this act but hands over to the social services department after taking out a place of safety order.

Unlike in a criminal court, it is not necessary to prove who caused the injuries but only that they were probably caused non-accidentally or, in the case of neglect or ill treatment, that someone failed to give the child the care and protection needed.

Composition of case conferences

Chairman—The person who chairs the conference is usually a senior member of the staff of the social services department. The recent draft from the Department of Social Security suggests that people in direct line management do not chair case conferences.

National Society for the Prevention of Cruelty to Children—Some staff attend as observers or consultants when they are directly concerned with the case. Officers in some areas have child protection teams. Some have family centres, nursery provision, and family counselling. The National Society for the Prevention of Cruelty to Children works closely with the social services department and provides lectures and training exercises for voluntary and statutory organisations.

Social worker and team leader—The social worker attending a case conference is usually the one who has carried out the investigation. The family's long term social worker may also be included. The social worker presents the background on the family, if known, as well as the current state. The team leader attends in support and as the social worker's supervisor. The team leader may help the chairman to ensure that everyone with relevant information on the case has been contacted or invited to the case conference.

Education welfare officer often attends case conferences and acts as a liaison for school staff and a link with the head teacher at reviews, etc. Increasing numbers of education welfare officers are becoming involved when a child discloses details of abuse to a member of the school staff. The officers may know the family already. The expectations of what they do in their everyday work varies among local authorities.

Police—Usually community affairs or juvenile liaison officers attend case conferences. Violence or sexual assaults on a child will often bring in the Vice Squad or Criminal Investigation Department, so all may attend. Police officers will usually give relevant information on any suspected person discussed at the case conference but will often not attend or give this information if parents attend the case conference. Police officers may have spoken to the child directly or interviewed the parents or suspected abuser. Serious assault on a child should be viewed as similar to that on an adult and the police informed so that the officers can investigate as soon as possible.

Health visitor, school nurse, nurse manager—Reports received or circulated will have the general practitioner's views if communication is good. Health visitors may take on a primary role after a case conference—for example, if the child is failing to thrive—by working on an agreed "contract" with the parents about diet, feeding, and attending clinics. School nurses are playing a more prominent part as more children tell of sexual abuse they have experienced within the family. The nurse manager attends to support the health visitor and school nurse and to be aware of decisions for supervising aspects of training of staff, etc.

General practitioners—The general practitioner is in a key position to make a vital contribution to the case conference, and the findings of the case conference are extremely important to the general practitioner. Though more case conferences are currently attended by general practitioners than was the case five years ago, it is still common for general practitioners not to attend a case conference. Some give verbal reports before the case conference, others use health visitors for conveying their opinion or some information. Other members of the case conference usually find the general practitioner's attendance helpful, and general practitioners usually learn a surprising amount about the family, which should be helpful.

Consultant or registrar may attend to speak, to report, and to participate in decision making.

Case conferences

Child abuse coordinator or adviser is usually responsible for the child abuse (child protection) register and is one of the few impartial members at the meeting. Such coordinators can ask objective questions and advise on criteria for, and standardisation of, decisions throughout the area. The role varies throughout the country. Such posts are usually funded by social services departments alone or jointly with the NHS.

Solicitor — A solicitor from the local authority may attend to give guidance to the case conference.

Occasional members as appropriate — A clinical medical officer working in the community (for example, at a child health centre or as a school doctor) may attend case conferences. Such doctors work at the interface between health, social work, and education services and will often be involved with children in adverse circumstances. A teacher or teachers may be asked to attend a case conference, including a teacher of a sibling of the child being discussed. When the child attends day nursery or nursery school a nursery teacher may be asked to attend. When the family receives benefit a member of the social security department can be extremely helpful; sometimes some stress can be eased by sorting out financial and debt problems. Similarly, when there are housing problems a member of the housing department may be helpful. The family may be overcrowded, in arrears with rent payments, or about to be evicted. Appropriate help may be considered by the housing department if the case conference recommends it. Members from voluntary agencies — for example, the Family Service Unit, Catholic Welfare, Dr Barnardo's — and statutory services such as the probation service may also be helpful at a case conference. Statutory and voluntary agencies will generally give priority to recommendations made by case conferences.

Both general practitioners and hospital doctors may claim a standard fee (advised by the BMA) for attending a case conference.

Although not a statutory or rigid meeting, the case conference is formal and is usually viewed as a valid and responsible form of communication and decision making. The minutes are usually available to the local area review committee and are circulated to concerned professionals, even when they are not present.

Case discussions

The other type of meeting usually arranged when there is concern for a child is a case discussion.

Case discussions are much more informal than case conferences and can be called by any professional who recognises that they would be useful for a few concerned people — possibly including the parents — to meet and hear what others know of the problems and difficulties.

A typical reason could be a child who seems not to be progressing well but shows no clinical condition. There may be missing pieces of a jigsaw that someone could provide that will help, ranging from problems of childhood jealousy to sexual abuse. A case discussion can also be used if a child is failing to thrive, the parents could actively cooperate in feeding regimens or in accepting guidance on handling and playing with their infant.

Further reading

Jones DN, ed. *Understanding child abuse.* London: Hodder and Stoughton, 1982.
British Association of Social Workers. *The management of child abuse.* Birmingham: BASW, 1988. (Available from BASW, 16 Kent Street, Birmingham B5 6RD.)
Department of Health and Social Security and Welsh Office. *Working together. A guide for inter-agency cooperation for the protection of children from abuse.* London: HMSO, 1988.
Standing Nursing and Midwifery Advisory Committee of the Department of Health and Social Security. *Child protection: guidance for senior nurses, health visitors and midwives.* London: HMSO, 1988.

PROTECTING THE CHILD

Barbara Mitchels

Child abuse appears in many diverse forms, entailing not only sexual but also physical or mental stress and often including cruelty or neglect.

Recent events have highlighted the problems faced by everyone concerned with cases of child abuse: the needs and welfare of the child are balanced against the rights of parents and the legal requirements of the courts. Often there are conflicts of interest that prove extremely difficult to resolve. Doctors, lawyers, and social workers need to work together to protect the child, having first established that there is a real need for that protection.

Legal procedures currently available to protect abused children are summarised below. The new Children Bill 1988 currently before parliament sets out to clarify and reform existing child care legislation. Proposals for reform are set out in the figure on the next page and are described in the text.

Note of warning on examination of children

A doctor (or anyone else) has no legal right to examine a child without the consent of a parent, guardian, or other person with parental rights or powers. This can cause problems when abuse is suspected and a medical examination is vital to establish whether such abuse has occurred.

When a parent or guardian brings a child to a doctor, for whatever reason, there is implied consent for a medical examination, and the doctor may then proceed to examine the child. It should not be necessary to seek further explicit permission to examine a particular part of the child.

If, however, permission is refused or withdrawn a doctor may find himself or herself in difficulty. A parent who withholds medical aid for a child may, however, render himself or herself liable for breach of the statutory duty to protect the child; a court order may override parental wishes in the child's best interests, and a local authority may consent to examination of a child in its care.

The Children Bill clarifies this grey area by enabling the court to give directions as to medical or psychiatric examinations when emergency protection orders and interim care or supervision orders are made. Emergency protection orders will be obtainable within a very short time after an event causing concern.

Place of safety order

When there is reasonable cause to believe that grounds exist that if proved would justify a care order, application can be made by any person (usually social services) to a magistrate or juvenile court for an order that a child be removed to and kept in a place of safety. The order lasts 28 days and is renewable.

The bill replaces this order with an emergency protection order, which would last for an initial maximum period of eight days, renewable once only for a further seven days.

Warrant to search for and if necessary to remove a child

Anyone acting in a child's interest may apply to a magistrate for a warrant when there is reasonable cause to suspect that the child has

Currently available legal procedures to protect children, with sequences of action

Legal procedures to protect children

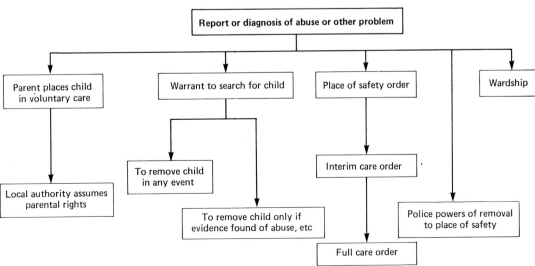

Protecting the child

Changes in child care law

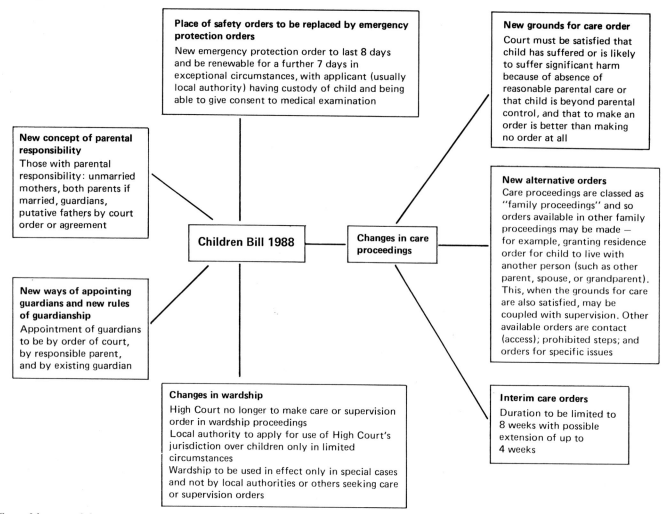

Place of safety orders to be replaced by emergency protection orders
New emergency protection order to last 8 days and be renewable for a further 7 days in exceptional circumstances, with applicant (usually local authority) having custody of child and being able to give consent to medical examination

New grounds for care order
Court must be satisfied that child has suffered or is likely to suffer significant harm because of absence of reasonable parental care or that child is beyond parental control, and that to make an order is better than making no order at all

New concept of parental responsibility
Those with parental responsibility: unmarried mothers, both parents if married, guardians, putative fathers by court order or agreement

New alternative orders
Care proceedings are classed as "family proceedings" and so orders available in other family proceedings may be made — for example, granting residence order for child to live with another person (such as other parent, spouse, or grandparent). This, when the grounds for care are also satisfied, may be coupled with supervision. Other available orders are contact (access); prohibited steps; and orders for specific issues

Children Bill 1988

Changes in care proceedings

New ways of appointing guardians and new rules of guardianship
Appointment of guardians to be by order of court, by responsible parent, and by existing guardian

Changes in wardship
High Court no longer to make care or supervision order in wardship proceedings
Local authority to apply for use of High Court's jurisdiction over children only in limited circumstances
Wardship to be used in effect only in special cases and not by local authorities or others seeking care or supervision orders

Interim care orders
Duration to be limited to 8 weeks with possible extension of up to 4 weeks

Some of the proposed changes in child care legislation: Children Bill 1988

been or is being assaulted, ill treated, or neglected in a way likely to cause ill health or unnecessary suffering or that one of certain specified offences is being or has been committed in respect of that child.

There are two types of warrant. The first allows the police to search for the child but to remove him or her only if the suspected ill treatment is found to exist; the second allows the police to remove the child in any event.

Magistrates have power to direct a doctor to accompany the police when executing the warrant, and usually the person who asked for the warrant will go too.

Police power to remove a child and keep him or her in a safe place

If the police have reasonable cause to suspect that circumstances exist that would justify a place of safety order or that a child is in the custody of a vagrant (someone with no settled home or an uncertain and erratic lifestyle, for example, a tramp) its officers have the power to remove that child without a warrant.

There is the safeguard that the station officer or an inspector must investigate the case as soon as practicable and either return the child or make suitable arrangements, usually with social services, for taking the child to a place of safety. Parents or others with parental rights must be

made aware of the procedure and of their legal rights. This protection lasts for only eight days, and parents may apply to a magistrate for the child's release.

The bill permits the removal of a child in specified circumstances, with additional safeguards, into police protection but for a period limited to 72 hours, during which an emergency protection order may be sought.

Wardship

Anyone with a personal interest in the welfare of a young person under 18 may apply to the High Court to make that person a ward of court.

The applicant must go to the principal registry of the family division of the High Court, which in London is at Somerset House and elsewhere in England and Wales is the local district registry, to complete a form called an originating summons, which details the names of the young person (minor), the other parties to the application — that is, parents, social services, guardians — the date of birth of the minor, and where the minor is to be found, if known.

Another form, the statement of claim, has to be completed. It should outline the matters on which the applicant requires the adjudication or direction of the High Court. This would usually include requests that the minor be made a ward of court, that care and control of the minor be given to a specific person or to social services, or possibly an order that the minor be returned to the care of a person from whom they have been taken. It may ask for an injunction to prevent the removal of a child from the country as an emergency measure. In such a case a photograph of the child may prove useful.

The procedure outlined above automatically makes the minor a ward of court for up to 21 days, during which an application must be made for an appointment to hear the case. This hearing will usually be before a registrar (a member of the judiciary junior to a judge), who will decide on preliminary or agreed matters and on evidence. The case might come back before the registrar or be heard before a judge, depending on its complexity. The minor remains a ward of court until otherwise ordered.

If no application is made within the 21 days the wardship lapses.

Wardship vests the legal control over the warded minor in the court. Parents and local authorities alike may make representations to the court, but the court retains legal control, delegating the day to day care of the ward to the most appropriate person. That person will then be able to consent to medical treatment on a day to day basis but would have to obtain the consent of the court for unusual or non-therapeutic medical procedures such as an operation for sterilisation.

The paramount consideration is always the welfare of the child, and all the court's decisions are made on that basis. Everything concerning the child, for example, education and housing, must be referred to the court, and the minor may not be taken out of the country or marry without the court's consent.

Emergency action in wardship

When there is a threat to the child an injunction can be granted for his or her protection forbidding the threatening act. This can be done "out of hours" and very quickly by contacting the duty judge through the High Court or the local district registry. A "port stop" may be effected to prevent a child leaving the country.

The bill makes a radical change in wardship proceedings by removing the power of the High Court to place a ward into the care or under the supervision of a local authority. This is an attempt to protect children and families from compulsory care or supervision except in cases in which statutory grounds for care proceedings exist under the bill and to preclude intervention by local authorities unless the child is likely to suffer significant harm. In the future if these proposals are implemented, wardship will be used less often and only in cases in which there are special circumstances justifying the intervention of the High Court.

Care proceedings

Interim orders

An interim care order lasting up to 28 days can be obtained during a place of safety order or police detention or by application to a magistrate or to the juvenile court. The juvenile court may make further interim orders if necessary.

The bill limits the duration of interim care orders to eight weeks, after which there may possibly be renewals up to a maximum of four weeks.

Full orders

Under the provisions of section 1 of the Children and Young persons Act 1969 the local authority, the police, or an authorised person may bring a child before the juvenile court for care proceedings on one or more of six grounds.

(1) The child's proper development is being avoidably prevented or neglected, his or her health is being avoidably impaired or neglected, or he or she is being ill treated.

(2) Another child in the same household is subject to a full care order or a person with a conviction for a specified offence is or is about to become a member of the household.

(3) The child is exposed to moral danger.

(4) The child is beyond the control of parent(s) or guardian(s).

(5) The child is not receiving sufficient full time education suitable to his or her age, aptitude, and ability.

(6) The child is guilty of an offence, excluding murder or manslaughter.

In addition, the child is in need of care and control that he or she is unlikely to receive unless an order is made.

The child, parents, foster parents, probation officer, local authority, and guardian must be informed of the proceedings, and the court must have access to information about the child's schooling, health, background, and character to make a fully informed decision.

A care order will last until the child is 18 (or 19 if the order was made when the child was 16 or over) or until the order is discharged.

The effect of a care order is to place the child in the care of the local authority, which then has parental powers and duties over the child for the duration of the order. The authority has control over the day to day care of the child and over access.

Under the provisions of the bill the grounds for making a care or supervision order will be simplified. The court must be satisfied that the child concerned has suffered significant harm or is likely to suffer such harm and that the harm is attributable either to the standard of care given (or likely to be given) to the child, being below that which it is reasonable to expect, or that the child is beyond parental control. "Harm" includes ill treatment, sexual abuse, and the impairment of physical or mental health or development. The courts have specific powers governing access to the child.

Supervision orders

The juvenile court can, on application by a person entitled to seek a care order (and on the same grounds), make an order placing a child under the supervision of the local authority for the area in which he or she lives. The High Court can also make a supervision order in wardship proceedings when the ward is not in the care of the local authority. The supervision will last for whatever time is ordered by the court or until the supervision is varied or discharged. There is a time limit of three years on supervision ordered by the juvenile court.

Supervision entails, in effect, exactly what its ordinary meaning implies—the overseeing of a child's progress by a named person or authority, but with the sanction that failure to comply would result in the supervisor bringing the matter back to the court for alternative protective measures to be considered. The court has power to add extra conditions to supervision—for example, residence with a specified person, attendance at a specified place for medical or psychiatric treatment, and attendance for intermediate treatment for a period of up to 90 days. Supervision orders may be changed or discharged by the court on an application by the child or supervisor. The bill provides that interim supervision orders may be made.

Assumption of parental rights

When a child is not subject to a care order but has been placed in voluntary care or abandoned, in certain circumstances the local authority can pass a resolution assuming parental rights over the child. Parents objecting may apply to the juvenile court for determination of the resolution. Unless determined, or rescinded, the resolution lasts until the child reaches 18 or is adopted. The proposed reforms remove the power of the local authority to assume parental rights by administrative resolution.

Comparative merits of the legal measures

The legal measures to protect children have different merits and uses.

Wardship is currently something of a sledgehammer. It is the most powerful and flexible but also the most complex and expensive procedure available. Usually wardship is used only in great emergency (perhaps when a child has been kidnapped by someone threatening to take him or her abroad) or when place of safety or care proceedings are inadequate or inappropriate. The delays in achieving a placement for a child tend to be longer in wardship proceedings. Time can be vitally important for a young and vulnerable child needing a settled home life. The proposed reforms will remove the power of the High Court to place a child into care or supervision in wardship proceedings, and therefore wardship will be used far less often in the future. A local authority can ask the High Court to exercise its inherent jurisdiction only with respect to children in cases in which there is risk of significant harm and the required result cannot be achieved by any other order for which a local authority may be entitled to apply.

Currently, in most cases a warrant for removal, coupled with a place of safety order and followed by care proceedings, will provide effective protection for a child. These are by far the most commonly used procedures.

When the present bill is enacted the normal protective procedures will be a warrant or police protection, allied to an emergency protection order and followed by interim or full care proceedings, or both, or supervision proceedings. Contact between child and parents will be presumed, with the courts having control. Contact may be prevented by court order in specified circumstances. In all cases the paramount consideration will be the welfare of the child.

Child care procedures in Scotland

Briefly, the main way in which child care procedures in Scotland differ from those in England and Wales outlined above is in the lower courts. High Court procedures differ in some respects, too, but are similar in principle. Conflicts of jurisdiction can arise, however, when a child's home is in Scotland but he or she lives in England.

In Scotland there are about 100 reporters (employees of the secretary of state). Two of the reporters' duties are to receive reports of child truancy, neglect, abuse, and any other matters affecting the welfare of children and to decide whether care proceedings are necessary. In appropriate cases they will call the child before a children's panel.

Each children's panel consists of three members of the public who have been selected and trained. They are volunteers, and they will decide each case on its merits, hearing evidence from the family, social services, school, and any other relevant source.

All decisions must be made in the best interests of the child.

The panel may order a discharge of the referral—that is, that there is no further action—supervision—that is, that the child stays at home but is supervised by a social worker—or a residential supervision order requiring the child to live in a special residential school or elsewhere away from home.

The panel's decision may be appealed against.

When care proceedings are not deemed necessary the reporter will arrange voluntary care, a formal warning, or require no further action.

The jurisdiction of the panel depends upon the acceptance by the child or parents of the grounds of referral, wholly or in part. If the grounds are denied the panel cannot proceed and it has to dismiss the case or refer it to a sheriff for proof. If the sheriff finds the grounds proved the case will be referred back to the panel for consideration.

The Children Bill does not reform child care law in Scotland or Northern Ireland.

Further reading

Bevan HK. *Child law.* London: Butterworth, 1989.
Department of Health and Social Security and Welsh Office. *Working together. A guide to arrangements for inter-agency co-operation for the protection of children from abuse.* London: HMSO, 1988.
Feldman L. *Care proceedings.* London: Longman, 1988.
Feldman L, Mitchels B. *The Children Act 1989—a practical guide.* London: Longman (in press).
Levy A. *Wardship proceedings.* London: Longman, 1987.
Mitchels B. *Child care and protection.* London: Longman, 1989.
Zentar R. *Practitioners' guide to child care law.* Manchester: Manchester Polytechnic, 1989.

MEDICAL REPORTS

Roy Meadow, Barbara Mitchels

Notification

A doctor who is worried that a child has been abused will telephone the local head of the social work department, whether in the hospital social work department or a community district. It is wise to follow up the conversation with a brief letter stating the cause of concern so that there is no chance of it being forgotten. The letter, marked confidential, may be brief but should be written in language understandable to a non-medical person.

Medical reports

Formal reports are required by the courts whenever medical evidence is being used in child abuse or child custody cases. Great care must be taken over the construction of the report so that your opinion is clear. Sometimes a solicitor will ask you to address particular issues in detail but quite often the doctor is asked merely for a "medical report."

- The report should be typed in double spacing with wide margins. It is useful to number the paragraphs or sections consecutively so that they can be referred to easily during discussion or in court.
- The document should be headed Medical Report and dated. The child's name, date of birth, and age at the time of writing should be written beneath.
- At the start give your full name, current position, and medical qualifications. Follow that with some indication of previous experience—for example, "I have been a principal in general practice for 12 years" or "I am a paediatric registrar who has worked with children for five years." If you have had particular training or experience of child abuse mention its extent; if you have published research work on the subject say so.
- Make clear the nature of your interest in the case in terms of how you came to encounter the child and how long you have been concerned with the case and in what capacity. State the extent of your knowledge of the case in terms of correspondence and discussion with colleagues and the nature of the documents and reports that you have seen. Sometimes many hospital records and documents will have been studied, in which case a statement such as "I have studied the case notes and relevant documents" is sufficient.
- State the extent of your contact with the child—for example, "I examined the child in my outpatient clinic and discussed the problems with the parents. The consultation lasted 50 minutes" or "I assessed the child every month during the following year, each assessment lasting about 15 minutes."
- Summarise the case, being careful to amplify any medical jargon as the report will be read by many non-medical people and will probably be seen by the child's parents. Terms such as petechiae or apnoea need explanation. When relating the clinical history write it down chronologically and in addition to the date make clear the child's age at each incident.
- Clinical findings follow the history and should be set out in an ordered fashion. A diagram or photograph may be added to supplement the description. When the pattern of injury is typical—for example, finger marks showing a firm grip on a child or slap marks—an explanation of how that pattern is recognisable is helpful to lay people. Though the main findings may relate to a particular injury or to just one part of the body, always include a general appraisal of the child, including his or her height and weight (and their centile value) and a note on the child's developmental abilities. This should be followed by a note of the child's behaviour during the consultation or at any other times that you have observed the child with the parents or elsewhere.
- The conclusion or opinion should be clear but not too dogmatic. The court wants to know your opinion and if possible to quantify it. Remarks such as "the findings are compatible with" can be extraordinarily unhelpful, and you should try to give an indicator of likelihood in terms of probability. State the reasons for your opinion in the report and be prepared to discuss them subsequently. Any confirmatory pathological or x ray findings should be reported, explained, and interpreted.
- If you have seen a statement from the mother or another party that contradicts your opinion finish your statement by making clear which of your findings are consistent with the contradictory statement and which are not, making any relevant comments arising from those contradictions.
- Date the report and sign your name at the bottom and keep a copy of the report for yourself because you will be questioned about it.
- For a court hearing seven or eight copies of the report may be required—for example, one each for three magistrates (or one if there is a judge), one for the clerk, one for the advocate (solicitor or barrister) for the council, one for the child's advocate, and one for the parent's advocate. It may also be helpful for the relevant social worker

to have a copy. The number of copies should be discussed with the solicitor concerned. Reports are often disclosed in advance, but if there are additional copies available you can decide at court after consultation whether it is appropriate to hand them out.

• Expert witnesses have additional roles. The duty of the expert may include an explanation of child development, child behaviour, and the effect of adverse factors such as abuse on the child. Thus the expert is drawing attention to the particular needs of the child for the benefit of those who have less experience with children. The expert witness may sit through the hearing to advise upon the different evidence presented. He or she may also be asked before the hearing to assess all the evidence and interview the family in order to present an authoritative opinion at the hearing.

Police reports

In some cases of child abuse the police will ask for a formal report. This needs to be on a police reporting form, which is available from either the local police station or the police officer who has asked for the report. Police officers like to come with their notebooks and write the report themselves and then present it to the doctor to sign. Many doctors do not like this because they find that the report they are asked to sign is written in language that they would not use ("I proceeded to the ward where I ascertained that the minor was in bed and commenced my investigation") or which does not quite reflect the opinion that they want to give (and would give if writing it themselves). Therefore most doctors prefer to write their own police report on the approved paper and send it to the police station. Sending the report by post allows more time for necessary thought and preparation. A hastily written report may be harmful to the case and also to the reputation of the expert. Under no circumstances should a doctor give in to pressure from the police or any other agency to prepare a report too hastily. The police officers will make it clear which areas of information they want in the report. Police reports are usually much briefer

than the lengthy medical report that may be required for court hearings.

Writing a report for the police does not necessarily mean that a prosecution will follow. Once the police have completed their investigation into alleged criminal offences the file is submitted to the Crown Prosecution Service for consideration of the evidence and for legal advice. When the evidence is sufficient the crown will prosecute the case on behalf of the police.

The Director of Public Prosecutions has a different function. When certain serious criminal offences are suspected the director has the power to initiate an investigation into the matter and to authorise prosecution in the public interest.

Affidavit

An affidavit is a statement of evidence set out in a standard format that has evolved over many years and is approved by the courts. It has to be sworn, or declared, before a commissioner for oaths or other authorised officer (which includes all solicitors and some court officers); a small fee is payable.

Documents or copies of documents that are relevant to the case may become part of an affidavit as exhibits, and copies may be made for all the parties to the case and for the judge. If an expert is asked to prepare a report for a civil case the report (if it is to be used in evidence) will be put into the form of an affidavit by the solicitor for the party calling the expert witness and disclosed to the other side. The evidence may then be agreed, in which case the witness need not attend the trial and the affidavit can be read. Alternatively the evidence may not be agreed and the witness may be called to court to give oral evidence. Oral evidence of expert witnesses may then be limited to the reports that have been disclosed but not agreed, saving the court's time.

Further reading

Kind S. *The scientific investigation of crime.* Harrogate: Forensic Science Services, 1987.
Kind S, Overman M. *Science against crime.* London: Aldus Books, 1972.

ABOUT COURTS

Barbara Mitchels, Roy Meadow

Even a fool can ask a question that an expert cannot answer.   DR JOHNSON

In cases of child abuse evidence may be required from doctors in various courts. The police may prosecute the offender. The child may be the subject of care proceedings, or the child's parents may seek a court ruling on domestic issues arising from the incident.

Doctors may be called, like anybody else, as ordinary witnesses to fact—for example, when they just happened to see a road accident—but more often they are called to court as professional witnesses in relation to one of their patients, giving evidence of fact on matters arising from their professional capacity as a doctor. Sometimes a doctor not necessarily connected professionally with the case is also called in as an expert witness to give an opinion or interpret facts using specialised knowledge and experience. The distinction between a professional and an expert witness is blurred, and the courts expect all doctors to use their medical skill fully and to give an opinion based on their observations, findings, and research using reference works, notes, diagrams, and other relevant material if appropriate.

There are proposed reforms in child protection law currently before parliament in the Children Bill, which may come into effect soon, although possibly not all at once. The bill alters some things, including the grounds for child care proceedings, but, although a new family court was suggested elsewhere, the bill leaves the court system unaltered for the moment, except for a few procedural alterations. The bill provides that care cases shall be heard in the domestic section of the magistrates' court, the county court, or the High Court. There will be a system devised to decide which court will be appropriate for each case.

The High Court is forbidden to make care orders within wardship proceedings and limitations are set on the use of its inherent jurisdiction relating to children in other proceedings. The main body of care work will then be done in the domestic section of the magistrates' court, with some cases of greater complexity or seriousness going to the county court and the High Court.

Doctors will appear mainly in the magistrates' court or the crown court in criminal prosecutions and in the domestic section of the magistrates' court, the county court, or the High Court in care cases and civil proceedings. For those who are called to give evidence it helps to know the set up of the courts, how to address those present, and a little about the differences in procedure.

Care proceedings court

Currently most care proceedings take place in the juvenile court. The new care proceedings courts will probably be similar. The court room is informally set out. At one end sits a "bench" of three specially trained magistrates (the chairman will be the one sitting in the middle); their clerk, a legally trained adviser, sits in front of them, and in from of him or her are tables or desks for the lawyers concerned with the case, the social workers and others, the parents, and the child. Anyone not directly concerned with the case is excluded from the court. The press is allowed to be there, but reporting is restricted and the child may not be identified in any way.

Ordinary witnesses have to remain outside the court until their evidence is required. The reason for this is that they should not be influenced by the evidence of others. Expert witnesses are an exception to this rule and may sit through the case until their evidence is called and remain thereafter if they wish. It is very useful to hear the evidence of other experts, together with the general evidence, to get a clear picture of all the relevant issues. Sit near the instructing advocate (solicitor or barrister) if possible—advocates may need a helpful word of advice as they conduct their case.

As a matter of courtesy, silence is observed in court during the proceedings by all who are not actively taking part. The court will take a dim view of whispered conversations at the back, so unless a matter requires urgent discussion it is better to pass a note or go outside to converse. If something needs to be communicated to advocates try to attract their attention unobtrusively and they can, if necessary, ask the court for a short adjournment to deal with it or

ask the court to pause for a moment while they take instructions.

There are no hard and fast rules as to whom professional or expert witnesses may speak before the case. Doctors may wish to confer with each other, and they can usually do so easily, but it is courteous to confer in the presence of their respective instructing advocates. It also shows the parties to the case who may be feeling vulnerable that they are not being "stitched up" by the experts. If speaking to a non-medical witness to ascertain some vital information is absolutely necessary it should be done through, or in the presence of, the appropriate advocates as there must be no question of possible influence being brought to bear by anyone on another's evidence.

During the case it is wise to consult your advocate about the propriety of discussions with another witness or party.

The court has to find the case proved on a balance of probabilities, and rules exist about the evidence that may be produced to satisfy the burden of proof. The most tricky to deal with is "the hearsay rule," which prevents witnesses giving evidence of any events that did not occur in their presence and also (with some exceptions) from relating to the court anything that was said by another person to them. In child care cases this rule of evidence is relaxed because the court needs to get at the truth and because sometimes a chance remark or admission may be germane, particularly in cases of abuse. When a doctor needs to quote a fact from medical records, possibly referring to an incident noted by a colleague, it would normally fall foul of the hearsay rule as the incident quoted did not occur in the witness's presence, but there are exceptions, with safeguards, to enable such evidence to be given in court.

Criminal proceedings

Criminal cases are tried in the juvenile court (if the accused is under 17), magistrates' court, or crown court.

Appeals from the magistrates' court on matters of fact are heard in the crown court by way of a retrial, and appeals from the magistrates' court on matters of law are heard in the divisional court of the Court of Appeal by way of case stated — that is, without hearing the live evidence again.

Appeals from a trial at the crown court pass usually to the Court of Appeal (criminal division) and then on a point of law of public importance to the House of Lords.

In criminal prosecutions resulting from alleged child abuse doctors will be called mainly before the magistrates' or crown court. The burden of proof in criminal trials is to satisfy the court beyond reasonable doubt that the accused is guilty of the crime alleged. As the accused's liberty and reputation are probably at stake the standard of proof is higher and the rules of evidence are therefore more strictly applied. The Police and Criminal Evidence Act 1984 governs the procedures for interviewing suspects, the taking of intimate samples from suspects, and

much of the preparation and presentation of evidence in court. Unlawfully gained evidence may be excluded.

Doctors may therefore find themselves in court giving evidence about examination of either a victim or a suspect, and it is important to remember that the rules for each are different. Examination of a child for evidential purposes must currently be with the consent of a parent, or guardian, or of social services when a place of safety or care order places the child in the care of a local authority. After the Children Bill comes into force medical or psychiatric examinations may require the consent of the court. Examination of a suspect must be in accordance with the provisions of the Police and Criminal Evidence Act 1984.

In the magistrates' court the layout of the court room and the bench is similar to that described in the juvenile court but more formal. The accused will be in a dock, possibly guarded, and the court room will usually have specific areas in which advocates, the public, the police, and others in the cases will sit during the proceedings.

The public is allowed into court, and the press present may report the case, with safeguards, provided that the child's identity is not disclosed.

Crown court

Criminal prosecutions in the crown court follow the same rules of evidence as those outlined above for trials in magistrates' courts. The trial will, however, take one of two possible forms. If the plea is guilty the hearing will be before a judge, whose task is to hear the facts of the case outlined by the prosecution and the mitigation for the accused and to sentence the offender after considering the circumstances of the offender and of the offence, together with any reports presented to the court. If it is a contested case the judge will sit with a jury. The jury will be the arbiters of fact in the case, and the role of the judge is to advise the jury on matters of law and evidence and to sentence the offender if he or she is found guilty, again after full consideration of the circumstances and available reports. Sentence may be delayed to obtain any further relevant reports required.

When the trial is by jury the court may seem rather theatrical to witnesses and onlookers. The images of Perry Mason or Marshall Hall may affect behaviour and attitudes unless carefully watched. It is tempting to want to impress the 12 people in the jury box with your knowledge, personality, or persuasive speeches, and their rapt attention to the evidence is very flattering. But bear in mind that they are people who are doing their best to understand the issues in the case and that they need a clear and concise explanation of the facts and opinions given. They are unlikely to be impressed for very long by meaningless waffle. The judge certainly will not be impressed at all and may well intervene if a medical witness seems to be going off the point.

The waiting rooms in crown courts are often better than those in the magistrates' courts, and there is usually a canteen to keep you going

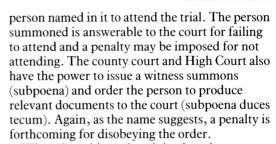

Courtyard and entrance (below) of Royal Courts of Justice, London

during the seemingly eternal wait to be called. The trials are usually longer in the crown courts, and the court may be less willing to make special allowances for expert witnesses to get away quickly, although most do their best to accommodate doctors, knowing that they have many pressing demands on their time.

Telephones are usually available for public use.

Be well prepared for trials by jury, making sure that you have sufficient copies of diagrams, documents, or reports to be used in evidence for the judge, clerk, and the jury, as well as for the advocates and the parties to the case. Medical records and clinical notes are not usually copied, for obvious reasons. Though they may be needed for the doctor's own reference, they would not usually be handed over to anyone else, unless the judge gives a specific direction.

Civil cases and care proceedings in county court and High Court

Most civil cases are tried in the county courts or the High Court, civil division. The case of the plaintiff (person bringing the action) must be proved on a balance of probabilities and the rules of evidence observed. After the Children Bill is enacted care cases will be heard not only in the domestic section of the magistrates' court but also in the county court and the High Court. It may become possible to move proceedings from one court to another, but the appropriate procedures for transfer and the way in which the venue for the start of care proceedings is to be decided are yet to be laid down in rules to be made by the Lord Chancellor.

The county courts have judges, and also registrars (rather like junior judges), who deal mainly with the preliminary pretrial issues and some non-contested cases.

Evidence in the civil courts is given either orally or by affidavit, or sometimes both ways.

If an expert is asked to prepare a report for a civil case the report will (if it is to be used in evidence) be put into the form of an affidavit by the solicitor for the party calling the witness and then be disclosed to the other side at or after the pretrial review of the case before the registrar. The evidence may then be agreed, in which case the witness need not attend the trial and the affidavit can be read; if, however, it is not agreed the witness may be called to court to give oral evidence. Oral evidence of expert witnesses may then be limited to occasions requiring elucidation or cross examination, saving the experts' and the court's time.

Going to court

Many doctors ask if they have to go to court if asked to do so. In a criminal trial if any person is in possession of facts that are material to the case to be heard before the court, and the court is persuaded that their evidence is both relevant to the issues and vital to the case, the court may order the person to attend as a witness. The court may issue a witness summons, which requires the

person named in it to attend the trial. The person summoned is answerable to the court for failing to attend and a penalty may be imposed for not attending. The county court and High Court also have the power to issue a witness summons (subpoena) and order the person to produce relevant documents to the court (subpoena duces tecum). Again, as the name suggests, a penalty is forthcoming for disobeying the order.

When the evidence is opinion based on observations after an event—for example, the findings on interview of a suspect by a clinical psychologist after an alleged confession to a serious crime—the question arises whether the expert may be forced to come to court and in what circumstances. An expert could be called in by the defence in the course of preparation of a case and prepare a report that proves unfavourable to the defence case. At this stage the defence may decide not to call that witness. It may choose to have the witness in court to assist in the conduct of the case, possibly by suggesting questions in cross examination, but not to ask that expert witness to give evidence. There is no duty to disclose an unfavourable report to the prosecution. But note that section 81 of the Police and Criminal Evidence Act 1984 enables the Crown Court to require either party to disclose to the other any expert evidence to be adduced in the proceedings. Any such evidence not so disclosed may not be adduced without the leave of the court.

Giving evidence

It is usual to stand when giving evidence but you may be asked whether you wish to sit. By tradition, advocates rarely sit and as it is easier to communicate with someone who is in the same posture as you; standing at ease but not easy is probably best.

In the magistrates' court replies to questions from an advocate should be directed not to the advocate but to the bench, speaking to the chairman. When speaking to one magistrate about another, perhaps referring to a remark or question from another person on the bench call the other "your colleague." In county courts or the High Court speak to the judge.

Do not be rushed, and be prepared to use the medical records before answering a question.

Any relevant notes, diagrams, and photographs or radiographs may be referred to in giving evidence. If the notes—for example, medical records—have been made by someone else they may be used if they form part of a continuous record and were made by people who have no personal interest in the case. If photographs or radiographs are challenged the advocate may need to call the person who took them to formally produce them in evidence. Charts, reference works, and tables may be used if necessary.

Aim to be concise and clear. Speak loudly enough for everyone to hear and slowly enough for the stenographer or judge to take notes. It is better to speak too slowly than too fast. It is better to speak too loudly than too softly.

Forms of address

- My Lord or My Lady: Lords of Appeal (sitting in the House of Lords); Lords Justices (sitting in the Court of Appeal); High Court judges or any deputy sitting as a High Court judge; and all judges sitting at the Central Criminal Court (the "Old Bailey")
- Your Honour: all circuit judges sitting in the crown court or the county court; recorders; and most other judges in the Commonwealth or United States
- Sir or Madam, or less commonly now, Your Worship: magistrates

It is customary to stand and bow to magistrates or judges when they enter or leave the court room. Similarly, when you enter or leave a court that is in session a modest bow to the bench or judge is appropriate

Keep your answers brief and do not volunteer long explanations unless asked for them.

Dress neatly and soberly. Behave with dignity (not pomposity); be courteous but not ingratiating.

Do not give opinions on subjects on which you do not have the relevant information or experience.

Occasionally you may have to put up with sarcasm, simulated anger, and obtuseness from an advocate, but keep cool and keep your answers correct and pertinent.

If an advocate starts quoting a contradictory opinion from a medical textbook and asks if you have heard of that textbook (or scientific paper) ask to be allowed to study the piece, particularly its context, before answering the question. If necessary the court will adjourn to allow you to do so. The advocate will rarely know the subject well enough to understand what is truly relevant and the witness should carefully consider the advocate's point before explaining why the question or piece of information is not relevant to the matter in hand. Bear in mind that some advocates during cross examination present a welter of questions and comments that are not always the result of detailed and relevant research but are merely provocative ammunition. There is no need to be upset by the welter of material; simply consider every question and dispose of each one appropriately.

If you do not know the answer to a question say so briefly and succinctly: "I do not know" or "No"; it is unwise to make excuses for yourself unless you are asked for them. Being in court is rather like the viva in an examination. It pays to listen carefully to the question and to answer only the question. Put first things first and do not bring in extraneous matter or subjects about which you know little.

As a medical witness your role is to serve neither the prosecution nor the defence but the court. When the court is considering child abuse your duty is to the welfare of the child. On this basis a doctor should be above any partisan feelings and not influenced by any matter other than the welfare of the child. All questions should be answered with this in mind.

Expert witnesses have additional roles. The duty of the expert may include explaining child development, child behaviour, and the effect of adverse factors such as abuse on the child. Thus the expert is drawing attention to the particular needs of the child for the benefit of those who have less experience with children.

As with all speaking engagements, first and last impressions count. Therefore, remember that at the start everyone will be watching and listening to you and similarly at the end when you leave the witness box. Make a good exit, picking up your notes efficiently before bowing to the judge or magistrate. Expert witnesses may wish to remain to the end of the case, but if not the court will usually release them promptly. If the advocate has not asked for you to be excused from the court ask the magistrate, "May I be released? I can be reached by telephone and return if the court wishes."

In their efforts to be fair to all parties court proceedings are subject to many adjournments and delays. The court officers are, however, considerate of doctors' time and make every effort to call their evidence as soon as possible. When you are asked to attend court it is useful to have your diary available and to specify particular times or days when it is difficult to attend because of clinical commitments.

The British Medical Association produces for its members a leaflet (No 33) which provides guidance on legal fees and allowances.

Anyone interested in fostering relationships among the legal, scientific, and medical professions should contact the membership secretaries of the following three societies.

- Forensic Science Society: Clarke House, 18A Mount Parade, Harrogate, North Yorkshire HG1 1BX (0423 506068)
- Medico Legal Society: Miss E Pygott, 1 Finsbury Avenue, London EC2M 2PJ (01 377 9191)
- British Academy of Forensic Sciences: Dr P J Lincoln, Department of Haematology, The London Hospital Medical College, London E1 2AD (01 377 7076).

ABUSE: THE EXPERIENCE

Sylvia Fraser

*These extracts have been compiled by Sylvia Fraser
from her book "My Father's House: A Memoir of
Incest and of Healing," by permission of Virago
Press, the publishers in the United Kingdom. The
book tells a story which is common. For many years
Sylvia Fraser thought that she was an ordinary
person until incestuous memories returned, at which
stage she feared she was a freak. The recognition that
sexual abuse within the family is common was, in a
strange way, a comfort; she realised that she was still
an ordinary person. She makes clear that the denial
in her family was a reflection of the denial in the
society that bred us all—a microcosm of the
macrocosm. Today's incest victims are merely
shouting the obvious for those who care to hear: "the
emperor has no clothes."—RM*

My father's house was a three storey, frame
building on a shady street in Hamilton, Ontario.
Though our family found it hard to grow grass
because of maple roots, our lawn was always
neatly trimmed, our leaves raked, and our snow
shovelled. No one drank in my father's house, no
one smoked, and no one took the Lord's name in
vain. Though my father worked on shifts at the
Steel Company of Canada, he always wore a white
shirt, navy suit, and tie to his job as a steel
inspector—trace memory of a family that had
once been prosperous. I was born into my father's
house on March 8, 1935. . . .

I sit on my daddy's lap playing tick tack toe
under the glare of a fringed and faded lamp. I
have the Xs, he has the Os. I get three across:
"I'm the winner!"

There's not much room on my daddy's lap
because of his big tummy, held up by a black belt.
His tummy feels warm against my cheek. The
buttons on his shirt are pearly in the light. I run
my fingers down them singing: "Tinker, tailor,
soldier, sailor."

My sister, Helen, who is four years older, says:
"When you run out of buttons that's the man you
have to marry!"

Twice every Sunday my family drives to St
James's United Church in my daddy's
secondhand Ford-with-a-running-board. I wear
white stockings and carry my Dionne Quintuplet
handkerchief with a nickel tied in one corner.
That is for the collection. My father and three
other gentlemen carry the silver plates tramp
tramp tramp up to the altar where Reverend
Thwaite blesses them, "Thank you, Fatherrr,
forrr yourrr bountiful blessings." He means God.

We drive home past the statue of Queen
Victoria with a bird's nest on her head and the 16
storey Pigott building, which I know to be the

tallest in the world, with my daddy honking every
time we get stuck behind a belt-line streetcar. At
the foot of Wentworth Street he points to a pile of
weathered boards on the side of the Mountain.
"That's where the old incline used to run."

I know by now he means a cable car that once
ran on a track to the top. Pressing my face against
the glass, I stare at this heap of boards, buried in
undergrowth. Try as I do, I can make no
connection between what I see and the wonder in
my daddy's voice. Yet his reverence for things
that once were and can never be again inspires my
favourite name, the one I use to baptise my oldest
and dearest friend: Teddybear Umcline.

Down down down the stairs I go, dragging
Teddy Umcline by one ear. My daddy sits framed
in his doorway in trousers and undershirt. As I
scuff my running shoe over the brass strip
marking the threshold, he puts out his black
shoe, which he has trouble reaching because of
his tummy. I get down on my hands and knees to
tie his lace. My daddy smells of Lifebuoy soap.
He rubs his face against mine. That's a whisker
rub. "You're tickling me!"

My daddy plays with my blond hair. "I had
curls like that when I was your age." He plays
with my belly button and jiggles pennies in his
pocket. My daddy squeezes my legs between his
knees. I count my pennies, already imagining
them to be black balls and red liquorice from the
Candy Factory. The breeze through the window
smells of lilacs. It blows the curtains inward like
Rapunzel's golden hair, giving me goose bumps.

My daddy and I share secrets.

My mother sprinkles my father's starched
white shirts with water from a vinegar bottle. She
is reciting a story I know ends with a mouse
piping: "Gee whillikers, an owl's egg!" I rock on a
hamper of freshly washed clothes, pretending to
listen but really worrying if I'll be smart in
school.

My grade one teacher is Miss Warner, who is
like a barrel with no neck and no waist. Arlene
Goodfellow says once when Miss Warner was
giving the strap her pants fell down to her ankles!

I am the first to learn all the voices of the vowels
and to read the adventures of Dick and Jane and
Spot and Puff through to the end. In the
cloakroom I teach the other kids to tie their
shoelaces in a double bow just like my daddy
taught me.

My daddy plays with my belly button, my
daddy plays with my toes as he did when I was
little: "This little piggy, that little piggy. . . ."
Now I lie on my daddy's bed, face buried in his

55

feather pillow. I shiver, because the window is open, the lace curtains are blowing, and I haven't any clothes on. My daddy lies beside me in his shorts and undershirt, smelling of talcum, He rubs against me, still hot and wet from his bath. My daddy breathes very loudly, the way he does when he snores, and his belly heaves like the sunfish I saw on the beach at Van Wagners. Something hard pushes up against me, then between my legs and under by belly. It bursts all over me in a sticky stream. I hold my breath, feeling sick like when you spin on a piano stool till the seat falls off. I'm afraid to complain because daddy won't love me won't love me love me.

I cry when my mother puts me to bed. I didn't used to be afraid of the dark but now I know that demons and monsters hide in the cubbyholes by my bed. I'm afraid one will jump out at me, and rub dirty dirty up against me with its wet-ums sticking out. I beg my mother to stay with me but she says, "Such a fuss!"

I have a scary night. My pillow tries to smother me with its dead feathers. When I wake up I am facedown in vomit. It smells like chicken guts.

Desperation makes me bold. At last I say the won't-love-me words: "I'm going to tell my mummy on you!"

My father replaces bribes with threats. "If you do, you'll have to give me back all your toys."

I tote up my losses: my Blondie and Dagwood cutouts, my fairytale colouring book, my crayons! "My mummy gave those things to me. They're mine."

"I paid for them. Everything in this house belongs to me. If you don't behave I've a good mind to throw them into the furnace."

I think of my beloved Teddy Umcline, his one good eye melting in the flames. "I don't care! I don't care! I don't care!"

"Shut up! What will the neighbours think? If you don't shut up I'll. . . I'll. . . send you to the place where all bad children go. An orphanage where they lock up bad children whose parents don't want them any more."

"My mother won't let you!"

"Your mother will do what I say. Then you'll be spanked every night and get only bread and water."

That shuts me up for quite a while, but eventually I dare to see this, too, as a game for which there is an answer: "I don't care. I'll run away!"

My father needs a permanent seal for my lips, one that will murder all defiance. "If you say once more that you're going to tell I'm sending that cat of yours to the pound for gassing!"

"I'll. . . I'll. . . I'll. . . ."

The air swooshes out of me as if I have been punched. My heart is broken. My resistance is broken. Smoky's life is in my hands. This is no longer a game, however desperate. Our bargain is sealed in blood.

I lie on my stomach on the living room rug, colouring in my fairytale book. I colour the hair of all the princesses with my yellow crayon— Cinderella and Sleeping Beauty and Rapunzel.

My father sits in his fetch-me chair working a crossword puzzle. His pencil snaps. He grunts: "Fetch me a paring knife."

I colour Cinderella's eyes blue, then turn the page to Sleeping Beauty.

"I'm talking to you!"

I colour Sleeping Beauty's eyes blue.

The floor trembles under my tummy. "Fetch me a paring knife."

I shuffle to the kitchen, s-t-r-e-t-ching the seconds like a rubber band, enjoying the terrible tension while wondering when it will snap. I hand my father the knife with the blade toward him, then return to my spot on the floor. With a black crayon, I outline the naked bodies of Cinderella and Sleeping Beauty and Rapunzel, right through their clothes, repeating ME ME ME. Then MINE MINE MINE.

Staring at my father's black boot, I boldly form the thought: I hate you . . . God does not strike me dead. I do not turn to stone. I repeat: hate hate hate hate hate, enjoying the sharp taste of the word like a lozenge in my mouth.

My arms stick to my sides, my legs dangle like worms as my daddy forces me back against his bed. I love my daddy. I hate my daddy. Love hate love hate. Daddy won't love me love me hate hate hate. I'm afraid to strike him with my fists. I'm afraid to tell my mummy. I know she loves Helen because she is good, but she doesn't like me because I am dirty dirty. Guilt fear guilt fear fear dirty dirty fear fear fear fear fear fear.

One day I can stand it no longer. I unscrew my head from my body as if it is the lid of a pickle jar. From now on there will be two of me—a child who knows, and a child who dares not know any longer. She will be my daddy's sexual accomplice. Though we will share the same body, I will not know of her existence. I will not experience, or remember, anything she does with daddy, and my loss of memory will be retroactive. I will not remember my daddy ever touching me sexually. I will not remember ever seeing my daddy naked. I will not remember my daddy ever seeing me naked. In future whenever my daddy approaches me sexually I will turn into my other self, and afterwards I will not remember anything that happened. This memory block will last 40 years.

INDEX

Index